WORLD WAR II

HISTORY OF WARFARE

Mike Sharpe

RSVP
**RAINTREE
STECK-VAUGHN**
PUBLISHERS
A Steck-Vaughn Company

Austin, Texas

www.steck-vaughn.com

Steck-Vaughn Company

First published 1999 by Raintree Steck-Vaughn Publishers,
an imprint of Steck-Vaughn Company.
Copyright © 1999 Brown Partworks Limited.

Library of Congress Cataloging-in-Publication Data

Sharpe, Mike, 1970–
    World War II / Mike Sharpe.
        p.   cm. — (History of warfare)
    Includes index.
    Summary: Recounts the causes, significant battles, and events of World War II, including background on the major political and military figures of the war.
    ISBN 0-8172-5451-X
    1. World War, 1939–1945--Juvenile literature.   [1. World War, 1939–1945.]   I. Title.   II. Title: World War Two.   III. Title: World War 2.   IV. Series: History of warfare (Austin, Tex.)
D743.7.S43   1999
940.53--dc21
                       98-44185
                       CIP
                       AC

Printed and bound in the United States
1 2 3 4 5 6 7 8 9 0 IP 03 02 01 00 99 98

Brown Partworks Limited
Managing Editor: Ian Westwell
Senior Designer: Paul Griffin
Picture Researcher: Wendy Verren
Editorial Assistant: Antony Shaw
Cartographer: William le Bihan
Index: Pat Coward

Raintree Steck-Vaughn
Publishing Director: Walter Kossmann
Project Manager: Joyce Spicer
Editor: Shirley Shalit

Front cover: Polish and German troops in battle, September 1939 (main picture) and a German motorcycle in North Africa, 1941 (inset).
Page 1: The ruins of Monte Cassino, Italy, after its capture from the Germans in May 1944.

Consultants
Professor Ken Hamburger,
American Military University,
Manassas, Virginia

Dr. Niall Barr, Senior Lecturer,
Royal Military Academy Sandhurst,
Camberley, Surrey, England

Acknowledgments listed on page 80 constitute part of this copyright page.

CONTENTS

INTRODUCTION

World War II remains the most violent and destructive conflict in human history. It lasted from 1939 to 1945 and when it was over large areas of the world had been devastated. About 15 million soldiers had been killed—along with 35 million civilians. Some six million of these were murdered in Nazi Germany's death camps. The scale of the military casualty list reflects the length and extent of the war, but also the weapons used.

Land warfare involved few weapons that had not been used in World War I (1914–18), but they were much more deadly in World War II. The key change on land was that the internal combustion engine became more reliable. Armored vehicles and trucks became larger and faster. Artillery, as the war progressed, also became much more mobile. Soldiers had their own mechanized troop-carriers, so they could move dozens of miles each day. Movement and firepower became the cornerstones of military success.

Ordinary soldiers also gained greater defensive firepower. They were given a light-weight weapon, the armored vehicle "killing" rocket, like the U.S. bazooka, which allowed them to deal with tanks.

At sea, changes were much more radical. The battleship, though still important, gave way to two vessels—the submarine and the aircraft carrier. The age of warships slugging it out within view of each other was ending. Naval battles took place without the rival fleets meeting head-to-head, as aircraft could fly many miles to attack a surface target, and submarines could lurk beneath the surface ready to fire a torpedo at an unsuspecting enemy vessel.

The most dramatic changes came in aircraft and air warfare. In 1939 some pilots were flying aircraft not greatly different from those of World War I. By 1945 a few were flying the world's first jet fighters or large bombers able to travel great distances to hit a target. Soldiers were also being flown into battle for the first time, either in gliders or dropped by parachute.

One of the greatest changes in warfare, due largely to radio communication, was the effective coordination of land, sea, and air forces in amphibious landings. The war in the Pacific was won because of such attacks, and D-Day, the invasion of occupied Europe in 1944, remains the largest amphibious operation of all time.

Because war was becoming more technological and soldiers needed more equipment to fight battles, there were increasing numbers of serving men and women who did not fight directly. Their job was to get soldiers into battle and keep them fighting. Estimates suggest that every man in action needed four or five others to support him with food, clothing, weapons, ammunition, and medical services.

World War II was brought about by the aggression of Germany and Japan, and it took until 1945 to crush them. Japan surrendered only after the use of the atomic bomb, which remains, with the exception of the hydrogen bomb, the most powerful weapon available today.

THE ORIGINS OF WORLD WAR II

The origins of World War II can be traced back to the Treaty of Versailles in 1919, which ended World War I, and to the rise of aggressive regimes in Germany, Italy, and Japan during the following years. Versailles was harsh on defeated Germany and in the 1920s many Germans began to resent the treaty. Adolf Hitler rose to power in Germany on the strength of this resentment. He was determined to make Germany master of Europe. The war that his policies engineered in 1939 proved to be the most brutal in history.

At the Versailles talks German politicians were forced to accept what were seen by many Germans as unreasonable terms. Germany was stripped of its colonies, the German fleet and armies were reduced to a shadow of their previous strengths, and Germany was forced to sign an admission that the outbreak of the war was its sole responsibility. Expensive reparations (payments in compensation for war damage) imposed by the treaty crippled the German economy in the early postwar years.

A humiliating peace treaty

These terms horrified and angered a large proportion of the German population. The victorious British and French were held responsible for the ruin of Germany. Territory Germany gained in the Franco–Prussian War (1870–71) was returned to France. The independent state of Poland, including West Prussia, which had been part of Germany, was created. A narrow strip of land linking the Baltic Sea with Poland cut off Eastern Prussia from the rest of Germany. In all, Germany lost about 13 percent of its pre-World War I lands.

The Versailles settlement was deeply humiliating to many Germans. Partly as a result of this, political extremism grew quickly in postwar Germany as different groups sought to deal with the country's problems. Poverty, high unemployment, and violent clashes between various groups of political extremists threatened to bring Germany to its knees.

Adolf Hitler (standing, in car) takes the salute of his Nazi supporters during a political rally in 1938. Hitler became the dictator of Germany in 1933 and began to strengthen Germany's armed forces. His ambition was for his regime, known as the Third Reich, to take over Europe.

ADOLF HITLER

Adolf Hitler, one of the most evil characters in world history, the dictator who ruled Germany from 1933 until 1945, was born in Austria in April 1889. Hitler drifted around Vienna, the Austrian capital, between 1909 and 1913, developing his increasingly extreme political views and hatred of the Jewish people. His passionate interest in politics continued when he moved to Munich in southern Germany. In 1914 he volunteered to fight in World War I. Wounded on the Western Front, Hitler was later awarded one of Germany's highest military medals.

In the political turmoil of postwar Germany, Hitler emerged as a skilled speaker, delivering speeches to discontented ex-soldiers and workers. By 1923 he was the head of the extremist Nazi Party. Hitler led a failed uprising in Munich against the government and was imprisoned. Released in late 1924 after writing *Mein Kampf* (*My Struggle*), an account of his political opinions, he organized and strengthened the Nazi Party, continuing to attract support among various German groups until the Nazis had become one of the most powerful groups in the state by 1928.

On January 30, 1933, Hitler became the political leader of all Germany. In the following months he established a cult of the führer–the leader. All political opposition was suppressed, and Hitler began to rearm for the war that he believed was the only way to make Germany a great power.

In 1939 Hitler ordered the invasion of Poland, an attack that was followed rapidly by the conquest of much of mainland Europe. Hitler was not a great military strategist, however. His mistakes, frequent outbursts of temper, and irrationality led to numerous blunders. However, his all-powerful image continued to inspire the majority of Germans throughout the war. Blind loyalty to Hitler allowed many Germans to carry out barbaric acts against Jews, Slavs, and any group he decreed as racially "inferior" to those with "pure" German blood.

In 1945 Hitler watched his dream collapse around him. Soviet forces were in Berlin, the German capital, by April. On the 30th, Adolf Hitler and the wife of his last hours, Eva Braun, committed suicide. Germany surrendered a few days after their suicides.

One extreme political group was best able to take advantage of Germany's disturbed state—the National Socialist Germany Workers Party—the Nazis. The party, led by Austrian-born Adolf Hitler, a veteran of World War I, seemed to offer a way out of Germany's many problems. Hitler, who was a master speaker, drew increasingly large crowds to rowdy meetings, where he spoke with hatred against those he saw as causing Germany's difficulties. Jewish people in Germany but also abroad were sin-gled out for Hitler's racial abuse. Hitler also spoke out furiously against the politicians who ran Germany after World War I.

Creating a "pure" Germany

By 1933 the Nazis had achieved a powerful if not a majority posi-tion in German politics. Thanks to his political skills Hitler became leader of all Germany at the end of January, and set about creating a regime, known as the Third Reich, that he claimed would rule for "1,000 years." A key part of this new Third Reich was the creation of a German "master race." At the head of this race was a supposedly racially "pure" type of German. Jews, Blacks, Slavs—all were seen as inferior. For these and other groups deemed as "impure"—homosexuals, gypsies, and Communists—there was to be no place in Nazi Germany.

This new and expanding German master race would need space to live, so-called "lebensraum," in Eastern Europe. Hitler had written in his autobiography *Mein Kampf* (*My Struggle*) of the need for new lands. These would include Germany's pre-Versailles territories in Poland and elsewhere in central Europe, and eastward into the Soviet Union.

Nazi supporters hand out leaflets urging Germans to avoid Jewish-owned shops and businesses. Once in power the Nazis began their persecution of Jews and others by introducing laws that prevented them from taking part in everyday life. Later, Jews and other groups were herded into grim camps where they were starved, denied decent medical treatment, worked to death, or simply murdered outright.

THE SPANISH CIVIL WAR

On July 17, 1936, only five months after the election of a liberal government in Spain, a military uprising led by extremist army officers began in various towns around the country. The failure of these army officers, later known as Nationalists, to win power immediately, due to the opposition of workers and loyal military units, led to a bitter civil war.

Both the Nationalists, led by General Francisco Franco, and the pro-government supporters, known as Republicans, received considerable military aid from other European countries. The most

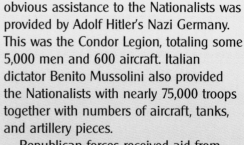

obvious assistance to the Nationalists was provided by Adolf Hitler's Nazi Germany. This was the Condor Legion, totaling some 5,000 men and 600 aircraft. Italian dictator Benito Mussolini also provided the Nationalists with nearly 75,000 troops together with numbers of aircraft, tanks, and artillery pieces.

Republican forces received aid from the Soviet Union. Volunteers from France, the United States, and Britain rushed to support the Republican cause. Nearly 40,000 foreign volunteers served in the Republican International Brigades, but they could not prevent the retreat of the Republicans from Spain's southern provinces and key cities.

By March 5, 1939, opposition to the Nationalists had just about disappeared and the Republican government fled into exile. The war cost the lives of nearly 500,000 people. It was also a testing ground for the new weapons and tactics that Germany and Italy were to use in Europe and Africa in World War II.

Foreign volunteers are disarmed by French troops as they flee over the Franco-Spanish border at the end of the Spanish Civil War.

Between 1933 and 1939 Hitler and the Nazis created a society controlled by various Nazi-dominated security forces. The strength of the German armed forces, which had been heavily restricted by the Versailles treaty, was also built up. At first this was done secretly but by the late 1930s large-scale rearmament was undertaken openly. New warships were built, and a program for training pilots for a coming war was vigorously promoted.

Hitler's aggressive attitude toward Czechoslovakia, an independent republic created at Versailles, became apparent in the mid-1930s. Czechoslovakia contained an area known as the Sudetenland, which had a majority of native German speakers. A Nazi-financed campaign caused unrest in Czechoslovakia. Few of the Western leaders had the will to resist Hitler's activities. The United States was following a policy of isolationism, avoiding becoming involved in overseas political affairs, and was in any case more worried about Japan, which was rapidly building up its armed forces. The British and French, still scarred by the horrors of World War I, were wary of provoking another war.

Approach to war

Hitler began to demand to take over the Sudetenland. The crisis over the Sudetenland reached a peak in September 1938, leading to the gathering of the major Western powers for a conference in Munich, southern Germany. The British prime minister, Neville Chamberlain, Prime Minister Édouard Daladier of France, Italian dictator Benito Mussolini, and Hitler were present. Hitler was given his way in return for peace in Europe and German troops were permitted to enter the Sudetenland. The conference was hailed as having prevented war.

European leaders attending the talks at Munich in 1938. From left to right: Italian dictator and ally of Hitler, Benito Mussolini; Adolf Hitler; Hitler's interpreter; and the British prime minister Neville Chamberlain.

With the Sudetenland, some of the most advanced arms factories in the world and huge stockpiles of raw materials had fallen into Hitler's hands. Some historians argue that the Munich settlement gave the Western powers a vital year in which to rearm, but Germany was better prepared for war in 1939 than it had been in 1938.

In March 1939 Britain and France issued a joint guarantee to protect Poland against Hitler, who was eager to take over Polish territory. Hitler's warlike intentions became obvious when he revoked the Non-Aggression Pact with Poland, an agreement designed to prevent war between the two that had been signed in 1934. After plotting some "border incidents" as an excuse for invasion, Hitler unleashed his armed forces against Poland on September 1, 1939. Britain and France were left with no other choice but to declare war on Hitler's Germany.

THE DAWN OF BLITZKRIEG

Between September 1939 and the summer of 1940, Nazi Germany's land and air forces stormed across Europe, and the victories they achieved stunned the world. Poland fell in 27 days, Denmark in 24 hours, Norway in 23 days, Holland in five, Belgium in 18, and then France in barely more than five weeks. After the defeat of France in June 1940, Hitler's armies stood poised on the coast of the English Channel ready to strike at Britain and complete the conquest of Western Europe.

Members of a Polish cavalry unit attempt to stem the advance of German tanks during the short campaign in September 1939. The speed and ferocity of the German invasion saw the Polish armed forces crushed in just four weeks.

The devastating effectiveness of German forces in 1939–40 was due in no small part to the tactical coordination of blitzkrieg. Blitzkrieg—"lightning war"—was not a new tactic, but few commanders fully understood it or knew how to counter it. The key to German successes during the early part of World War II was to combine the most powerful armored and air forces in the world. This was the cornerstone of blitzkrieg.

During the years between the end of World War I in 1918 and the outbreak of World War II, the blitzkrieg theory was widely taught in German military academies. The man who did most to promote the idea in Germany was General Heinz Guderian. Guderian rose to prominence while lecturing in the German army. His belief in rapid strikes at enemy forces won him many supporters, including Adolf Hitler. When the world's first large armored unit was created, Guderian became its commander.

Nazi Germany's first victories

By September 1939, the dawn of blitzkrieg warfare, Guderian had turned Germany's armored units into a highly skilled fighting force. The French had equal numbers of tanks as well armored and gunned as anything the Germans had, but France's generals were less advanced when it came to using tanks.

On September 1, 1939, Guderian's theories were put into practice. Of all the German forces that attacked Poland only one-sixth were armored or motorized

THE GERMAN BLITZKRIEG

The core of Blitzkrieg was a German panzer (armored) division with its tanks. Each division, however, was capable of dealing with most events that mobile warfare might throw at it. Each division had its own supporting infantry, engineer, antitank, artillery, and anti-aircraft units. Panzer divisions were highly mobile and powerful.

The panzer divisions were not generally supposed to attack an enemy's strongest points, but strike rapidly, driving through points of weakness, causing confusion and never allowing the enemy to regain the initiative. Major enemy defenses or large bodies of troops were avoided.

The speed of a panzer division's attack was greatly helped by the close support provided by the Luftwaffe, the German air force. Dive-bombers attacked enemy troop concentrations, headquarters, and key communication points, such as bridges, thereby making sure that the enemy had been "softened up" before the tanks, supported by artillery, attacked.

units. Nevertheless, after a sustained aerial and ground bombardment of the Polish defenses, it was these units that pierced the front. Fast, light tanks raced into the enemy rear unchecked by Polish aircraft, most of which had been destroyed on the ground by the Luftwaffe (German air force). German tank losses were heavy, however—over 80 percent of some types were lost to enemy fire or mechanical breakdown.

After the Polish campaign the Germans introduced major changes to their war production, ensuring that when the Germans invaded the Low Countries (Belgium, Luxembourg, and the Netherlands) in May 1940, the strike would be harder and faster. In the months after Britain and France's declaration of war on Germany on September 3, 1939, Germany's arms factories shifted their production to heavier, better-armored tanks. German commanders also emphasized the need to improve the flow of supplies—fuel and ammunition—to their tank units.

At dawn on May 10, 1940, lightning war was unleashed on Western Europe. Glider-borne German assault troops landed on the supposedly unconquerable Belgian fortress of Eben Emael,

The German invasion of France and the Low Countries in the summer of 1940. It was planned with great care. The Germans decided to bypass the Maginot Line, a series of fortifications defending France's border with Germany, which was supposed to stop any German invasion in its tracks. The bulk of the German armed forces was ordered to sweep through the forested, supposedly impassible Ardennes region north of the Maginot Line. They would then drive north to the English Channel. By doing this they effectively split the French and British forces in two.

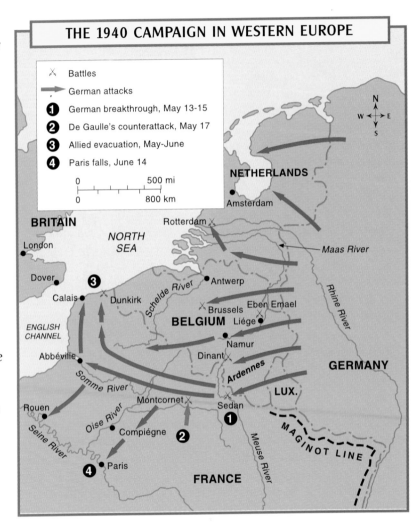

THE 1940 CAMPAIGN IN WESTERN EUROPE

Battles

German attacks

❶ German breakthrough, May 13-15

❷ De Gaulle's counterattack, May 17

❸ Allied evacuation, May-June

❹ Paris falls, June 14

situated close to the German border and a little way to the north of Liége. Belgium had not declared war on Germany after the invasion of Poland, but its neutrality did not suit Hitler or the general who planned the attack on France, Erich von Manstein.

As the attack on Eben Emael was taking place, German troops were also landing in the Dutch city of Rotterdam. At the same time, other German forces charged across the Dutch border and also headed for Rotterdam. To the south, two armored divisions roared across the Maas River and headed into Belgium. The British and French had expected this attack. The British Expeditionary Force (Britain's army in France) and several French armies moved north into Belgium to halt the Germans.

Unbeknown to the French and British, large German forces were also threading their way through the narrow forest roads of the Ardennes just to the north of the Maginot Line, a line of strong defenses along France's border with Germany that was supposed to prevent any invasion. The German armies simply bypassed the Maginot Line by moving through the Ardennes. These units included the majority of Germany's poweful armored divisions. Two of the armored divisions that moved through the Ardennes, one commanded by General Erwin Rommel, reached the Meuse River near the town of Dinant on May 13.

Bridges were constructed across the Meuse under heavy French artillery fire, and then the German tanks began their race across France. The speed of the advance was stunning. By May 15, a 50-mile (80-km) gap had been punched through the French defenses. Near Sedan, Guderian's armored division was moving so quickly that he was ordered by Hitler to slow down and then halt. The French fought bravely to stop the German drive to the English Channel coast. Near Montcornet, on May 17, Colonel Charles de Gaulle counterattacked the Germans, but his small force of tanks could make little impression.

Evacuation at Dunkirk

In Holland, Amsterdam fell with little fighting on May 15. The Dutch government's leaders had fled to London the previous day and surrendered their country. Five days later, the leading German tanks reached Abbéville on the French coast, thereby trapping the French and British forces in northern France against the English Channel. However, by this time the British Expeditionary Force was making plans for an evacuation back to Britain from around the port of Dunkirk.

The week after the Germans had reached Abbéville, the British forces fell into headlong retreat. Equipment was abandoned or sabotaged to prevent it from falling into German hands. Vast amounts of supplies were also abandoned. The evacuation, which was given the codename Operation Dynamo, began on

A photograph that appeared in a German propaganda magazine showing the commander of a tank. The magazine, Signal, was sold in those parts of Europe occupied by Germany. The intended message was that Germany had the military might and confidence to take over the whole of Europe if need be.

May 26. By June 4 some 338, 000 men had been brought to English ports in a rag-tag collection of warships, yachts, fishing boats, and pleasure cruisers. The evacuation was a significant moment in World War II. It allowed the British to continue the war against Hitler, and Britain would, in time, be the base from which the Allies would begin the liberation of Europe.

Having driven the British back across the Channel, the Germans headed south. On June 16 French leader Marshal Henri Pétain sued for peace. German forces took over northern France and installed a German-controlled government under Pétain in the south. It was called Vichy France after the town where the government was based. The Germans insisted that the French surrender at Compiégne, where the Germans had signed their surrender at the end of World War I.

Britain stands alone

In a brief campaign the Germans had conquered all of Western Europe. Only Britain and its far-flung empire remained to oppose Hitler's armed forces. Steeled by the speeches of Prime Minister Winston Churchill, Britain prepared to be invaded, but first Hitler had to win control of the skies over southern England.

The struggle in the skies over southern England, known as the Battle of Britain, was a close-fought event, and the first campaign in history that took place solely between rival aircraft. Throughout the summer of 1940 the Luftwaffe squadrons flying mainly from bases in northern France pounded Royal Air Force (RAF) airfields dotted across southern England. RAF Fighter Command had the significant advantage of an extensive early-warning radar system and a highly capable leader,

---

KARL VON RUNDSTEDT

Karl von Rundstedt was one of the most effective German generals during the invasion of Western Europe in 1940. He was popular with his men, who referred to him by the affectionate nickname of "the Old Gentleman." Rundstedt was born into a Prussian military family on December 12, 1875. By November 1914 he had reached the rank of major, and ended World War I as a staff officer.

In the following years he rose through the ranks but retired in October 1938. Eight months later he was recalled to active duty, and placed in command of a large number of German armies during the invasion of France in May 1940. His forces formed the southern arm of the pincer that encircled the British at Dunkirk. In 1941, Rundstedt led a large part of the German forces into the Soviet Union, but resigned in December.

After being recalled to active service once again in 1942, Rundstedt was given the task of stopping the invasion of Europe in 1944. He later planned the Ardennes counterattack, Germany's last offensive of the war, and the defense of the German border. Rundstedt was captured in May 1945. After spending three years in jail, he was released. He died in Hanover, Germany, on February 24, 1953.

Sir Hugh Dowding. Dowding made the most of his limited forces to repel the attackers. However, during August and early September the RAF was losing more pilots than it could replace, and its airfields were being hammered by German bombers.

The turning point in the battle came when Hermann Goering, the head of the Luftwaffe, switched his forces from attacks on the RAF's fighters and their airfields to the bombing of London. The British capital was beyond the range of the best German fighters and the German bombers were left unprotected. During September 1940, scores of German aircraft were destroyed. The people of London and other major British cities endured great suffering during what was known as the "Blitz," but these attacks on British cities gave the RAF time to regroup. Hitler decided to call off the invasion of Britain on October 12.

Some historians have argued that Hitler believed that an invasion of Britain was unimportant compared to his forthcoming attack on the Soviet Union. Hitler had always planned to conquer the Soviet Union, a country he hated and whose people he wanted to enslave. However, there is no doubt that the Battle of Britain was one of the crucial victories of the war as it ensured that Britain could be a launchpad for any future invasion of Nazi-occupied Europe. Hitler sent the bulk of his forces to fight the Soviet Union, leaving Western Europe less well defended.

One of the RAF's pilots prepares to board his Hurricane fighter at the height of the Battle of Britain. Although the Hurricane was not as modern as some enemy fighters, it was more than a match for the relatively slow and poorly armed German bombers.

HITLER TURNS EAST

In July 1940, while the Battle of Britain was being fought, Hitler began to plan a major invasion of the Soviet Union, despite having signed a non–aggression pact with the Russians in 1939, just before the German invasion of Poland. There were serious doubts about Hitler's decision among his senior commanders. But Hitler hated the Soviet Union, which he saw as the home of Communists and Jews. He wanted to extend German control over its lands, peoples, and resources.

German troops take shelter from enemy fire behind a Czech-built tank during the first weeks of Operation Barbarossa, the invasion of the Soviet Union, which began in June 1941.

Hitler's belief that he could crush the Soviet Union proved to be his costliest blunder. By invading the Soviet Union without defeating Britain, he was forced to fight on two fronts for the rest of the war. Germany could not take on the might of the Soviet Union and the Western Allies (anti-German forces) at the same time, particularly after the United States entered the war in 1941.

The plan to invade the Soviet Union was code-named Barbarossa after an old German hero, Frederick Barbarossa, and it was scheduled to last no more than four months. On the Allied

side most were in agreement that the invasion would succeed. Field Marshal Sir John Dill, Britain's Chief of the Imperial General Staff, gave the Soviet Union's Red Army a mere six weeks to hold out. Some British intelligence sources thought the Soviet Union would surrender in just ten days. Their fears were perhaps justified because the Soviet leader, Joseph Stalin, had many of his senior officers executed or imprisoned in the 1930s because he feared their power. To add to this shortage of trained officers, the Red Army was also poorly equipped and controlled by political officials with few military skills.

War on a grand scale

The German plan called for an attack along a 2,000-mile (3,200-km) front by Army Groups North, Center, and South. Each group, which consisted of a number of armies, was to be supported by air units. Ground units were pulled from all across German-occupied Europe, but with hindsight it is clear that they were ill-equipped for the task. Any attack would need motor vehicles, yet the Germans had too few, and many of those available were unlikely to function in extreme weather conditions. However, the Germans at first did not expect to have to fight through the winter.

The number of German armored divisions was doubled, but only by stripping the existing ones of half their tanks and pressing captured ones into service to form new units. Russia's rail network, which might have speeded supplies to German forward units as they pushed deeper into the Soviet Union, ran on a different gauge (distance between the rails) from that of Germany. German railroad cars could not be used in the Soviet Union.

PRISONERS OF WAR

During the initial German drive across Eastern Europe hundreds of thousands of Red Army troops were captured. The Geneva Convention, a series of regulations governing the treatment of prisoners, was recognized by most countries, but the contempt in which the Eastern European peoples were held by the Germans ensured that many of them were murdered outright or worked to death. Behind the German lines in Eastern Europe special units were detailed to execute Soviet prisoners, often thousands at a time. German prisoners could expect savage reprisals if they were captured by the Russians. Few Germans who went into Soviet prisoner of war camps ever returned to their homeland.

Other Allied prisoners fared better at the hands of the Germans. Most were sent to German prisoner of war camps, where they were usually treated according to the Geneva Convention. Conditions were far from luxurious, but at least the prisoners were dealt with reasonably fairly. The Red Cross was allowed to send them parcels with food and other everyday items.

A few prisoners of war in Germany escaped with the help of European resistance (anti-German) movements. One of the most notorious prison camps was Colditz, a vast granite castle in eastern Germany, which was filled with those who had tried several escape attempts.

Fighting in the Balkans, which diverted large German forces into southern Europe between March and May 1941, delayed the start of Barbarossa for a crucial five-week period. In fact, there were considerable advantages to the revised June 22 start, not least the favorable weather and long summer days.

At dawn on the 22nd, from the Arctic Circle to the Black Sea, an army of 3.2 million men advanced into the Soviet Union. The Luftwaffe devastated the great lines of Soviet aircraft that it caught on the ground. German armored units raced ahead as they had in France. Army Group Center drove toward Moscow capturing 300,000 prisoners and the city of Minsk on the way. The tank was the decisive weapon in the early days of the war, yet the German armored units found themselves facing a considerable enemy in the Russian KV-1 tank. It was well-armored and outgunned most German tanks—a sign of things to come.

In the weeks after the German attack, Soviet industry began to evacuate on a large scale from the western Soviet Union to areas behind the Ural Mountains, well beyond the range of the Luftwaffe. Between July and November 1941, over 1,500 industrial plants (1,360 of them armament manufacturers) moved farther east. The Russians were not going to give up without a fight.

Despite the speed of their advance, the Germans also found it necessary to commit large numbers of troops—men they could ill-afford to spare—to combat Soviet partisans (guerrillas) in conquered areas. By mid-July the Red Army had undergone great changes. Commanders were given more independence to make their own decisions, and the senior officers held in Stalin's prisons since the 1930s were released.

German tanks move cautiously through a Russian village at the beginning of the winter of 1941. It was often so cold that fuel for motorized vehicles froze and small fires had to be placed under the vehicles to get them moving.

Red Army soldiers launch an attack on a German outpost in the final battles of 1941. Unlike the Germans, most Soviet soldiers were supplied with warm winter clothing. These men wear lightweight winter camouflage smocks and trousers over their uniforms.

Hitler made a fateful decision to intervene in his generals' battle plans on July 19. He ordered two armored divisions involved in the main attack on Moscow to aid the secondary advances on Leningrad in the north and the Ukraine in the south. The German attack on Moscow was weakened.

The Russian winter closes in

The capture of the city of Kiev in the south on September 26 was only achieved after bitter fighting, but Hitler was determined to conquer the Ukraine, an important grain- and oil-producing region. As winter approached, the German race to Moscow intensified. Rains set in and mud created vast traffic jams. Temperatures fell quickly, catching the Germans unprepared. Few had been equipped with warm clothes. By November over 750,000 Germans had been killed, wounded, or taken prisoner.

By the beginning of December, Army Group North and Army Group Center had been driving toward their goal, Moscow, for five months and needed time to make vital repairs to their vehicles and bring up supplies. Hitler ordered a halt to operations on December 8. During the same week the Red Army launched a massive counterattack. These troops were from Siberia, where they had been placed to halt any Japanese attack on the Soviet Union. However, a Soviet spy in Japan had discovered that the Japanese had no intention of attacking the Soviet Union, so the Siberian troops could be moved to face the Germans without danger. By January 1, 1942, the immediate threat to Moscow had been lifted by the attacks of the Siberian forces.

By the summer of 1942 Hitler had become fascinated by the idea of capturing Stalingrad, a city on the Volga River named after the leader of the Soviet Union, Joseph Stalin. However, his forces were far too small and badly supplied to capture the city. The Germans reached the city by the last months of the year, but were unable to capture it. The Russians, sensing Germany's weakness, drew on their reserves of manpower and were able to inflict the first major defeat on Nazi Germany during World War II by January 1943. Stalingrad was a hard-fought battle, but by the end the Germans had suffered huge casualties. They were forced to give up many of the gains they had won during their first campaign against the Soviet Union in 1941 and the first half of 1942.

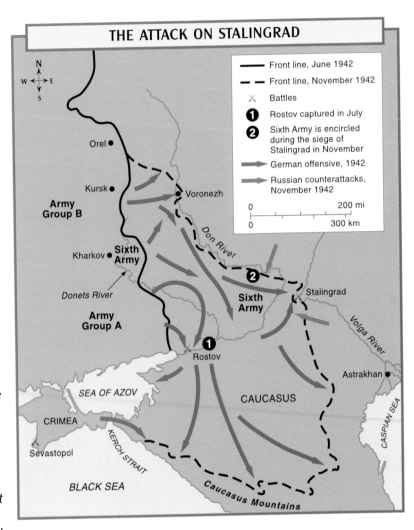

THE ATTACK ON STALINGRAD

Legend:
— Front line, June 1942
- - Front line, November 1942
✗ Battles
① Rostov captured in July
② Sixth Army is encircled during the siege of Stalingrad in November
→ German offensive, 1942
→ Russian counterattacks, November 1942

0   200 mi
0   300 km

The Red Army's counterattacks continued throughout January and February of 1942, but these attacks were thrown back at almost every point by the Germans. The situation deteriorated into a stalemate during the spring thaws, which made the movement of men or machines next to impossible. Hitler ordered his armies to hold their positions.

The push on Stalingrad

On May 8, the Germans renewed their onslaught to eliminate the gains achieved by the Red Army during its winter offensive. Substantial advances were made in the Crimea. Sevastopol, a key Soviet port, was captured by early July and some 100,000 Red

Army troops were killed. The brief rest that followed the German spring offensive was shattered by the opening of their summer attack on June 28. This was aimed at Rostov and Stalingrad, the gateways to the Caucasus and its oil fields. On July 13 Hitler decided to strike at both of these targets at the same time. By dividing his main force, he risked fatally weakening it and also created a vulnerable gap between the two new armies.

The drive on the Caucasus began on July 13. German troops quickly captured Rostov, but the advance on Stalingrad was slowed by the diversion of more forces to the south. Then, angered by the slow advance on Stalingrad, Hitler withdrew units from those forces earmarked to support the attack on Rostov and sent the units back to Stalingrad. The Rostov campaign, hampered by inadequate resources, ground to a virtual halt as all focus switched to the attempt to take Stalingrad.

A German catastrophe

Throughout the fall of 1942 the German Sixth Army fought in Stalingrad what its soldiers referred to as the "rattenkrieg," or "war of the rats." The bitter fighting in the rubble of Stalingrad was a nightmare. Every last yard was fought over. The Soviet defenders were prepared to fight a war of attrition—weakening and exhausting the Germans. Georgi Chuikov, the Soviet general defending Stalingrad, seemed to have almost limitless resources. General Friedrich von Paulus, commander of the German troops in Stalingrad, received few reinforcements.

On November 19, a Soviet counteroffensive drove around Stalingrad from the north and south and cut off the Sixth Army. German troops were trapped within the city they had tried to capture. General Erich von Manstein was ordered by Hitler to reopen a route into Stalingrad, but he failed. Hitler continued to refuse von Paulus permission to attempt a breakout, but when a key German-held airfield near Stalingrad fell to Soviet forces on January 22, 1943, the thin trickle of supplies that had been reaching the Sixth Army stopped completely. On February 2, von Paulus surrendered with 100,000 of his men. It was the decisive turning point of the war on the Eastern Front.

German troops wait for the order to advance amid the ruins of a tractor factory in the northern part of Stalingrad. So intense was the fighting that much of the city was leveled. The troops were left with little shelter to ride out the worst of the Russian winter.

THE WAR AT SEA

Perhaps some of the most important battles of World War II were fought at sea. Without the flow of supplies across the North Atlantic from North America, it is unlikely that Britain could have survived. If the Germans had taken control of the Mediterranean Sea, then Britain would have been cut off from its oil supplies in the Middle East and its forces in the Far East. The naval war also saw key changes in the importance of types of warships. Battleships were replaced as the decisive weapon by aircraft carriers and submarines.

As part of the Treaty of Versailles in 1919 naval expansion was limited in all the major sea powers. This was an attempt to prevent the arms race that had led to war in the late 19th and early 20th centuries. Germany and Japan ignored the restrictions and both built modern navies. The German navy, particularly its fleet of submarines, waged a deadly battle to halt the flow of Allied supplies across the North Atlantic from North America to Britain and the Soviet Union.

The Germans developed battleships, such as the *Tirpitz* and *Bismarck* and smaller but faster "pocket" battleships, such as the *Graf Spee*. However, their U-boats (submarines) were the most powerful underwater force in the world throughout the war. On the other hand, the Germans failed to built aircraft carriers.

A German U-boat cuts through a light swell as it heads out from its base on the west coast of France. It is making for the North Atlantic to sink Allied merchant ships.

The Battle of the Atlantic

The battle for control of the sea routes of the Atlantic was the longest and most crucial naval campaign of the war. Writing his postwar memoirs, Prime Minister Winston Churchill stated that it was the only aspect of the war that had genuinely scared him. The German navy commanders tried with every means at their disposal to destroy enough merchant ships to force Britain out of the war, and by mid-1942 they were dangerously close to victory.

The greatest threat in the early months of the war came from the modern surface raiders *Graf Spee* and *Scharnhorst*, but they sank relatively few ships and were most valuable in luring Allied warships away from the Battle of the Atlantic. *Graf Spee* was lost off Montevideo, Uruguay, in December 1939 and the *Scharnhorst* was sunk in December 1943.

The fall of Norway and France in 1940 changed the situation. German vessels could operate from Norwegian and western French ports. Losses of merchant shipping increased throughout 1940–41, when Britain was dependent on U.S. oil supplies. However, the British captured a German Enigma encoding machine, which was supposed to turn top secret messages into an unbreakable code. This gave the Allies access to enemy radio transmissions.

Despite this fact, in the spring of 1941 U-boats sank huge numbers of ships. The British Royal Navy was able to sink the *Bismarck* in May 1941, but U-boats were the great danger. Escort ships and basic air cover became available during the second half of 1941. A boost to British naval strength in the Battle of the Atlantic came when the United States leased the Royal Navy a number of destroyers.

Conquering the U-boats

Losses continued at a staggering rate through most of 1942. Improvements in technology, such as radar, better depth-charges, and the availability of long-range escort aircraft to force the U-boats to submerge (where they had a reduced running speed) gradually favored the Allied cause. But in November 1942 losses of shipping peaked. Britain had barely three weeks of oil and food left, and the situation grew critical.

Dreadful weather conditions slowed down U-boat operations in the early months of 1943, but the submarine attacks increased in the spring. In June, Allied anti-submarine tactics began to

THE U-BOAT ACES

Germany's U-boat submarine aces were afforded the same kind of reverence that was heaped on Britain's Royal Air Force pilots during the Battle of Britain. They were much praised at home, and feared abroad. The three most famous, Günther Prien, Otto Kretschmer, and Joachim Schepke, were all awarded the Knight's Cross with Oak Leaves, one of the highest awards given to German military personnel.

Prien earned his medal for a daring attack on a Royal Navy warship at anchor on October 14, 1939. Steering his submarine, U-47, through the defenses stretching across the harbor, Prien sank HMS *Royal Oak*, one of the Royal Navy's battleships. Kretschmer and Schepke, commanding U-99 and U-100, were credited with large numbers of enemy shipping sunk in the first 18 months of the war.

In March 1941, Prien and Schepke were killed, and Kretschmer was taken prisoner. Although U-boats continued to sink Allied vessels, their loss was the first of a number of body blows that wore down the German submarine force. The Allies also began to develop new weapons. Radar, when used with sonar, an underwater sound detector, heralded the end of the U-boats.

work more efficiently and U-boat losses rose dramatically. Seventy-four were lost in the next two months. With the U.S. shipping industry working at full capacity and able to produce a "Liberty" merchant ship in only five days because these freighters were made of prefabricated, easily put together sections on a production line, the tide turned. Although they remained a threat until the end of the war, U-boats were no longer such a danger.

Naval war in the Mediterranean

In 1940 the British maintained a large fleet dedicated to protecting Malta, Gibraltar, and Cyprus from where they could guard

THE CONVOY SYSTEM

The Allied convoys that plied across the Atlantic between North America and Europe and to Russia via the Arctic throughout World War II were the most vital link in the struggle in Europe as they brought over a huge percentage of the men, weapons, and supplies used to free Europe from Hitler's tyranny.

Before escort warships were utilized, the ships of the convoys, usually sailing in parallel lines, were at the mercy of the German U-boats and "pocket" battleships. Few merchant ships could reach more than a slow speed and sometimes had

to travel through a waiting line of German U-boats. The first indication of a U-boat attack on a convoy was often the explosion of a torpedo. In the middle of the North Atlantic, chances of survival for men in lifeboats were often slim, particularly in winter.

Once convoys began to be properly organized and protected by a screen of warships equipped to detect and sink enemy submarines, losses declined. Aircraft, either land-based or flying off small carriers also played a major role in ending the U-boat menace.

An Allied convoy and its escorting warships come under heavy attack from German and Italian aircraft as they sail through the Mediterranean Sea heading for the island of Malta.

the vital sea routes to the Mediterranean and to the Far East through the Suez Canal. When France fell in May 1940 and Italy declared war on the Allies, the British Royal Navy found itself engaged in another struggle. Significantly, the Italian navy had no aircraft carriers. In November 1940 the British used a handful of carrier-based torpedo-bombers to sink one Italian warship and badly damaged two others at anchor in Taranto harbor in southern Italy. It was a lesson in the power of naval aviation that influenced the Japanese attack on the U.S. Pacific Fleet at Pearl Harbor in December 1941 (see pages 30–31).

The need to support British forces in North Africa (see pages 26–29) seriously overstretched the Royal Navy, however. The Mediterranean is a small, enclosed sea and British ships operating in it could be attacked by German or Italian aircraft flying from their land bases. When Luftwaffe units began operating over the Mediterranean in the early months of 1941, British losses soared.

Malta in particular was subject to many attacks by bombers. The tiny, British-held island was a vital point between the western and eastern Mediterranean, where the entrance to the Suez Canal begins. It was also possible for British aircraft flying from Malta to attack German and Italian aircraft and vessels moving between southern Europe and Africa.

The British also deployed submarines against German and Italian shipping supplying their armies in North Africa, prompting the Germans to begin using Atlantic U-boats in their struggle. These caused great destruction and had seriously weakened the Royal Navy's warships in the Mediterranean by early 1942. Throughout that year, the Luftwaffe continued to savage British convoys and Malta, the only base open to the Royal Navy in the central Mediterranean.

When the tide of the conflict in North Africa turned in favor of the Allies in late 1942, the German and Italian warships were denied the use of forward bases from which to operate. This was perhaps the decisive aspect of the struggle in the Mediterranean, and by May 1943, Allied naval supremacy was reestablished.

The aftermath of the attack by British aircraft on the southern Italian port of Taranto on November 11, 1940. A handful of old British aircraft flying from a carrier used torpedoes to sink or disable seven Italian vessels. The attack was the first occasion when carrier aircraft were used to strike at enemy warships.

THE NORTH AFRICAN CAMPAIGN

When Italy, an ally of Germany, declared war on France and Britain in June 1940, North Africa, a region divided between Britain, France, and Italy, became a crucial theater of war. The immediate Italian target was the Suez Canal, a vital supply link between Britain and its troops in the Far East. Italian dictator Benito Mussolini also wanted to capture the British-controlled islands and colonies in the Mediterranean and North Africa. In September, Mussolini's forces invaded Egypt from nearby, Italian-run Cyrenaica (Libya), beginning a campaign that would last for nearly three years.

In early September 1940, a little over 35,000 British troops faced 200,000 Italians in the Western Desert, a vast barren area along the North African coast. General Sir Archibald Wavell, the British commander in the Middle East, justifiably feared his position. However, Wavell's opponent, Marshal Rodolfo Graziani, was not a man for bold moves. He refused to launch an offensive until Mussolini threatened to fire him.

On September 13, five Italian divisions advanced into Egypt from Cyrenaica. The British looked unlikely to survive the Italian invasion. The Italians advanced to Sidi Barrani, where they constructed a series of fortified camps. The British counterattacked on December 9, driving across the North African desert in a series of spectacular advances masterminded by General Richard

A British armored vehicle leads a huge crowd of Italian prisoners into captivity at the end of December 1940. Despite being heavily outnumbered, the British were able to virtually destroy the Italian armies in North Africa. However, their sweeping success led to the arrival of a much more dangerous foe in North Africa, Germany's General Erwin Rommel.

ERWIN ROMMEL

During the desert campaigns in North Africa, the victories that Erwin Rommel's forces achieved made him a great hero among the German population. Rommel was born in Heidenheim, Germany, on November 15, 1891. He was given a commission in the German army in 1912, and won his country's top award for gallantry, the Pour le Mérite, at the Battle of Caporetto, northern Italy, in World War I. During the interwar years he became an influential infantry tactician.

Rommel was given command of the Seventh Panzer Division in February 1940. A successful campaign in France during the following summer led to his appointment as commander of German forces in North Africa in February 1941. He won his reputation as a daring and skillful commander in the next 15 months, and was named the "Desert Fox" because he was so hard to pin down. After his defeat at El Alamein in November 1942, he was recalled to Europe and later ordered to prepare to defeat the Allied invasion of Western Europe. In October 1944 he was implicated in a failed plot by senior German generals to kill Hitler and was forced to commit suicide.

O'Connor. The Italians were defeated time and again. On January 22, 1941, the Italian fort at Tobruk, an important port, fell. The British had advanced 500 miles (800 km) and captured 130,000 Italian troops.

Attack and counterattack

Hitler had already decided that he could not permit the Italians to be crushed in North Africa and the first German units began arriving in Tripoli, Libya, on February 14. General Erwin Rommel was sent to command this desert army. Despite the small size of his forces, Rommel attacked the British line, whose vulnerable supply line stretched from the Nile River westward to Beda Fomm. When the attack came on March 21, 1941, the British bases at El Agheila, Agedabia, and Benghazi fell quickly.

The British were determined to prevent the vital port of Tobruk from falling into German hands. On April 10, the first attacks came. Tobruk was defended by 15,000, mostly Australian,

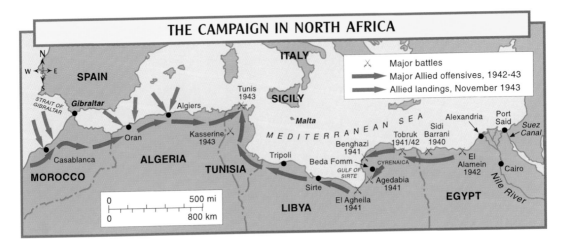

THE CAMPAIGN IN NORTH AFRICA

The fighting in North Africa between 1940 and 1943 took place along a narrow coastal strip. The German and Italian forces were trying to capture the Suez Canal. However, the huge distances involved meant that both sides had to capture or defend ports such as Tobruk. Without these ports supplies would have to travel overland, which was a far too slow process to really keep pace with high-speed warfare.

troops under General Leslie Morshead. The Australians repulsed repeated assaults and survived intense artillery and air bombardment. Most spent their time underground in bomb-proof shelters during the bombing. Rommel failed to capture Tobruk.

The campaign in North Africa ebbed and flowed across the North African coastal strip for the next year. Counterattacks by a succession of British generals forced Rommel away from Egypt but he always launched his own attacks, which in turn forced the British back toward Egypt. In late May 1942 Rommel's forces struck again, forcing the British to fall back into Egypt. Tobruk fell on June 21. Rommel began to advance from Tobruk toward Egypt on June 26.

Two battles at El Alamein

The British commander, General Sir Claude Auchinleck, decided to make a stand at El Alamein, barely 55 miles (88 km) west of Alexandria and near the Suez Canal. His troops dug in along a position defended to the south by the Qattara Depression. This low impassible desert area forced Rommel to make a frontal attack. By July 7, Rommel's forces had been halted.

Churchill replaced Auchinleck with General Bernard Montgomery on August 13. Rommel attacked Montgomery in the first week of September. By September 7, the German attacks had been called off. Rommel went to Germany on sick leave, and on October 23, 1942, Montgomery began the Second Battle of El Alamein. A huge artillery barrage pounded the German lines, prior to the advance of infantry through the enemy minefields. The fighting was locked in stalemate until November 3, when

Rommel (who had returned on October 23) ordered the withdrawal of his forces. Hitler demanded that Rommel halt the retreat on November 5. However, British pressure and Rommel's need to find a defensible line forced the retreat to continue.

The final blow against the Germans and Italians was struck on November 8, when over 100,000 U.S. and British troops commanded by U.S. General Dwight D. Eisenhower began to land in Algeria and Morocco. It was the first major involvement of U.S. ground forces in the war against Hitler. Algeria and Morocco were French colonies and under the authority of the German-controlled Vichy government in France. The U.S. and British forces had a considerable stroke of luck when the 100,000 Vichy troops surrendered without firing a shot.

The end of the fighting

The Germans were pushed back to within 30 miles (50 km) of Tunis by January 1943. Rain hampered further movement, so the Allies advancing into Tunisia from the west dug in to wait for reinforcements. Montgomery continued his advance along the coast throughout January and February. Rommel was able to inflict a defeat on U.S. forces at Kasserine in February, although the untried U.S. troops fought hard.

On April 22, the Allies attacked in force. Hitler replaced Rommel with General Jürgen von Arnim. He was in a hopeless position. Tunis fell on May 7, and by the 14th the remaining German and Italian forces in North Africa were in captivity.

A French soldier (second from left) gives directions to American and British troops outside a hotel in Algiers, the capital of Algeria, shortly after the successful Allied landings in November 1943.

JAPAN'S PACIFIC BLITZKRIEG

Relations between the United States and Japan had been worsening for some time before World War II. Japan's leaders wanted to create an empire that stretched across the Pacific. This would bring them into conflict with the United States. The Japanese saw that the U.S. would win a long war because of its industrial might, but they hoped to win one decisive campaign that would force the U.S. government to ask for peace. The main Japanese target was the U.S. Navy's base at Pearl Harbor in the Hawaiian Islands.

On the first day of December 1941 the decision was made to attack the U.S. Pacific Fleet anchorage at Pearl Harbor. It was a move that most Japanese commanders thought would bring the Americans to the negotiating table and give up their possessions at Wake Island, Hawaii, and the Philippines.

The air attack on Pearl Harbor began early in the morning of Sunday, December 7, a day chosen because it was estimated that a large part of the U.S. Pacific Fleet would be in port. The first wave of aircraft consisted of 183 dive- and torpedo-bombers, with fighters providing protection. They flew off six carriers that had sailed to within 250 miles (400 km) of the Hawaiian Islands. Although the aircraft were detected by radar operators, they were mistaken for some U.S. bombers that were expected.

U.S. naval personnel try to cut through the hull of the capsized Oklahoma, *one of the battleships sunk at Pearl Harbor, to reach the men trapped inside. The Japanese surprise attack on the base left 2,280 military dead and 1,109 wounded.*

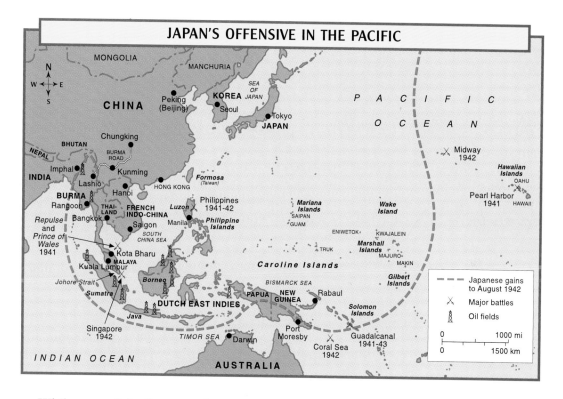

JAPAN'S OFFENSIVE IN THE PACIFIC

While part of the Japanese force attacked U.S. fighter aircraft that were parked at various airfields, the torpedo-bombers made runs across the anchorage toward the battleships lying off Ford Island in Pearl Harbor. Six of the battleships were soon sunk, sinking, or very badly damaged. A second wave of 167 aircraft attacked fuel stores and airfields. The Japanese believed that by sinking the battleships they had crippled the U.S. fleet. However, the U.S. carriers *Enterprise, Lexington,* and *Saratoga* were not at Pearl Harbor. As later events were to show, carriers and not battleship were to become the key warships in the Pacific theater.

Rapid Japanese victories

The Japanese attack on Pearl Harbor ensured that the United States would enter World War II. U.S. President Franklin D. Roosevelt addressed Congress on December 8. He described December 7 as a "day that will live in infamy." Congress voted to declare war on Japan, but not Germany and Italy. However, due to the alliance that Japan had with Germany and Italy—they were known as the Axis powers—these countries sided with Japan and declared war on the United States on December 11.

Between December 1941 and the summer of 1942, the Japanese launched attacks all across the Pacific. They had two aims: first, to establish a series of island bases to protect the territories they had captured; second, to secure areas that produced vital raw materials, such as oil.

Six hours after the Pearl Harbor attack on December 7, Japanese aircraft were bombing airfields in the Philippines, where General Douglas MacArthur was the chief U.S. military adviser. The bombing attacks were followed by an amphibious assault on Luzon, the main island of the Philippines. The defense of Luzon became legendary. The heroism and self-sacrifice with which 65,000 Filipinos and 15,000 Americans battled with the Japanese invaders in the hostile jungles of Luzon's Bataan Peninsula is worthy of that legend.

MacArthur was evacuated to Australia before Bataan fell in April 1942, vowing "I shall return." American prisoners in the hands of the Japanese were less fortunate. They were forced to march to camps in northern Luzon, and thousands died on the way. Many more died in the camps.

The British generals who surrendered Malaya and Singapore, Britain's main naval base in the Far East, to the Japanese on February 15, 1942, were completely outwitted by the Japanese. Only two hours after the attack on Pearl Harbor, forces led by

Japanese troops march through downtown Singapore after the British garrison had surrendered on February 15, 1942. Britain's defeat in Malaya remains the country's worst ever. Britain's casualties in Malaya, mainly men taken prisoner, totaled 138,700. In contrast, the Japanese suffered 9,824 men killed, wounded, or taken prisoner.

General Tomoyuki Yamashita had landed at Kota Bharu on the northeastern coast of Malaya. They then moved south, brushing aside British forces sent to block them. On December 10, the British suffered a major loss when the battleship *Prince of Wales* and the battle cruiser *Repulse* were sunk by land-based Japanese aircraft while trying to attack an invasion fleet off Malaya.

By January 10, 1942, Kuala Lumpur, one of Malaya's chief cities, was in Japanese hands and 17 days later the British had withdrawn to Singapore, an island a little way off the southern tip of the Malayan Peninsula. The assault on Singapore began on February 7. The Japanese crossed to the island under heavy fire. Outnumbered, the defenders fell back and a week later Singapore's water supply was in Japanese hands. On February 15, the garrison of 80,000 men surrendered.

The early months of the war brought Japan some equally stunning successes. By June 1942, the Philippines, Burma, Malaya, and Dutch East Indies were occupied. In the first months of the war, Japan had established a defensive island barrier around the Pacific and captured crucial raw materials (rubber and oil fields).

America strikes back

The first of the crucial naval battles of 1942 was fought between Japanese and U.S. forces on May 7–8 in the Coral Sea. This was part of a wider Japanese offensive, code-named Operation Mo, which aimed to establish bases for them for air attacks on the northeastern coast of Australia. Although the U.S. Navy carrier *Lexington* was sunk in the Coral Sea battle, one Japanese carrier, the *Shoho*, was sunk and two others were damaged so that they

The Shoho, the Japanese aircraft carrier sunk during the Battle of the Coral Sea, is struck by a torpedo on May 7. Two other Japanese carriers, the Shokaku and Zuikaku, suffered varying degrees of damage. The U.S. Navy had the carrier Lexington sunk and the Yorktown slightly damaged. Although the losses in the battle were roughly equal, the Japanese were forced to abandon their plans to invade New Guinea. Coral Sea was the first battle in naval history in which the rival fleets never actually met at close range. All of the attacks they launched used aircraft.

CHESTER W. NIMITZ

Texas-born Admiral Chester Nimitz was the leading figure in the naval strategy to defeat the Japanese in the Pacific during World War II. He was an officer with a background steeped in naval thought and experience. Nimitz attended the U.S. naval academy at Annapolis. During World War I, he served as the chief of staff to the commander of the navy's Atlantic Fleet.

Shortly after the Japanese attack on Pearl Harbor in December 1941, Nimitz was promoted to admiral and placed in charge of the Pacific Fleet. On March 30, 1942, Nimitz was promoted further. He was made commander of all naval and air forces in the Pacific. In this position Nimitz was responsible for overseeing the overall strategy that America followed to defeat the Japanese in the Central Pacific.

Nimitz handled his position with great skill and diplomacy, making sure that rivalries between the various commanders under his direction did not get out of hand and therefore undermine the war effort. He was involved in many of the major attacks in the Pacific, and the Japanese surrender in September 1945 was signed on his flagship, the *Missouri*.

were unable to take part in any immediate future operations. The Japanese abandoned the invasion of Port Moresby, the main settlement on New Guinea.

Between May and June, Japanese land and sea operations again attempted to push their defensive perimeter to the southeast, and to develop an airfield on the island of Guadalcanal. Once that was achieved, the Japanese planned to attack Port Moresby again. Despite the Japanese failure in the Coral Sea battle, Admiral Isoroku Yamamoto, commander of the Japanese Combined Fleet, thought he could destroy the U.S. Pacific Fleet under Admiral Chester W. Nimitz in one decisive action on the high seas.

The Japanese halted

Yamamoto chose Midway, an island some 1,000 miles (1,600 km) west of Pearl Harbor, as his battleground, and assembled a formidable force that included four large aircraft carriers. Unbeknown to the Japanese, U.S. intelligence experts had intercepted signals relating to the planned attack. When the Japanese fleet arrived off the northwest of Midway during the night of June 3, the Americans were fully prepared, with two fleets under Admirals Frank Fletcher and Raymond Spruance.

In a battle that began on the 4th and lasted until the 6th, aircraft from the *Enterprise*, *Hornet* and *Yorktown* sank the *Akagi*, *Soryu*, *Hiryo*, and *Kaga*. The U.S. lost the *Yorktown*. Again, the two fleets never came in direct sight of each other. In addition to the crippling loss of four of its best carriers, the Japanese navy had lost many of its aircraft and their most experienced pilots. The Americans were easily able to replace their losses of aircraft and crews, and had learned valuable lessons in the difficulties of coordinating warships and aircraft.

Encouraged by the victory at Midway, MacArthur and Nimitz began planning for the first American offensive of the war. Code-named Operation Watchtower, it aimed to secure communications with Australia, take the Solomon Islands and New Guinea, and capture the Japanese base at Rabaul on the island of New Britain. Until the end of 1943, fighting in the Pacific theater concentrated in this area at the southeastern edge of the Japanese defensive perimeter.

The struggle for Guadalcanal

Guadalcanal lies in a key strategic position in the Solomon Islands. If captured by the Japanese, it could have been used to cut the sea routes between the United States and Australia. At the end of May 1942, the Japanese had a limited military presence in Guadalcanal—less than 3,000 men. Importantly though, they were constructing an airfield, which could dominate the area if it became operational.

U.S. Marines take a break during one of many sweeps through the thick jungle of Guadalcanal in search of the island's Japanese garrison.

On August 7, a U.S. Marine division landed unopposed on Guadalcanal and captured the airfield the following afternoon. The U.S. Marines on Guadalcanal then faced a serious setback when a convoy carrying much of their equipment was forced to fall back after encountering Japanese warships.

The Marines were now on their own, and established a small defensive boundary with the few supplies of mines and barbed wire they had. There were few tools for digging, but equipment left behind by the fleeing Japanese enabled Marine engineers to finish the airfield, which the engineers named Henderson Field. By August 20, the first American aircraft were landing. However, two days earlier the first Japanese reinforcements were landed at a point 20 miles (32 km) east of Henderson Field.

Three days later an attack by the Japanese was repulsed and the force almost destroyed. On September 12, another attack was driven back by the Marines during what became known as the Battle of Bloody Ridge, located on the southern edge of the airfield's defensive perimeter. Thus a pattern of attack was established that continued until February 1943, when the Japanese finally abandoned Guadalcanal.

THE FIGHT
FOR ITALY

The decision to invade Italy in 1943 was not universally popular among the Allies. However, at a conference attended by Churchill and Roosevelt in January 1943, Churchill suggested that the Allies could effectively control the Mediterranean if Italy were occupied, and that by pressing the Axis on another front the Germans would be forced to divert troops to Italy from the Eastern Front and France. Churchill's suggestion was agreed to, and the invasion of Italy, by way of the island of Sicily, began in the summer of 1943.

A British officer (in peaked cap) confers with U.S. paratroopers from the 82nd Airborne Division in the square of a Sicilian town shortly after the Allied landing on the island in July 1943.

On July 10, 1943, some 180,000 men of the U.S. Seventh Army and British Eighth Army landed on the shores of Sicily, off the southwestern coast of Italy. Complete air cover was assured by 4,000 Allied aircraft. The Eighth Army, under General Bernard Montgomery, met with little opposition at its landing point just south of Syracuse. Resistance at the Gulf of Gela, disembarkation point for the U.S. forces, was stiffer but overcome.

Syracuse fell on July 12, but Montgomery's push to Messina on Sicily's northeastern coast slowed down in the face of determined German defenders. The U.S. forces, under General George Patton, were hampered by mountainous terrain, and he chose instead to make a looping attack around the northern coast, taking Palermo on July 22. U.S. troops reached Messina on August 22, shortly after the German evacuation across the Straits of Messina to the Italian mainland.

Invading the mainland

At the end of July Italian dictator Benito Mussolini had been placed under house arrest by members of his own government, and intelligence reports indicated to Allied leaders that the Italians would soon leave the Axis. However, the Germans freed Mussolini and reinstated him as a puppet leader. The Germans poured men into Italy. The Allies had lost the initiative and this was to cost them dearly.

BENITO MUSSOLINI

Benito Mussolini, Adolf Hitler's chief ally in Europe, was dictator of Italy from 1922 until his execution by his own countrypeople in 1945. Mussolini, who had come to power before Hitler, was much admired by the German leader, but their alliance was dominated by Hitler, with Italy very much the junior partner.

Mussolini kept his grip on power by dealing ruthlessly with any political opponents. He also built up Italy's armed forces, but they were unable to win him the overseas empire he desired. Italy's contribution to the Axis war effort was generally unsuccessful. In fact, German troops were often sent out to support Italian forces that were on the verge of collapse, especially in North Africa.

Public support for Mussolini among the Italian people waned as the war turned against the Axis alliance. By the time the Allies invaded Italy in 1943, Mussolini was a marginal figure with little support among the Italian people.

In August it was decided that it was time to invade the Italian mainland. So, on September 3, the British crossed the Straits of Messina and landed in Calabria. The landings were virtually unopposed. In contrast, the amphibious assault on Salerno by U.S. forces very nearly proved disastrous. The German defenders were easily able to predict the landing sites and the U.S. troops under General Mark Clark had to fight hard to establish a beachhead. The British plan was to drive through Calabria and link up with Clark, trapping the Germans in the process. The skill with which the Germans defended forced the Allies to rethink their plans, and the Germans escaped the pincer movement.

Superiority of numbers and command of the skies again proved the Allies' greatest asset and they slowly advanced north. Naples, a key port, fell on October 1, and the air bases around Foggia were in Allied hands by October 5. These were the two prime Allied objectives, as the latter brought Romania's oil fields, which supplied oil to Germany, within striking range.

At this point, Albert von Kesselring, the German commander in Italy, persuaded Hitler into changing his tactics of a slow withdrawal from Italy. Kesselring convinced Hitler of the value of a

defensive line, the Gustav Line, across the peninsula some miles south of Rome. The Allies continued their slow drive north on either side of the Apennine Mountains with winter approaching.

With hopes of an early victory dashed, the Allied commanders decided to capture Rome. The Gustav Line stood directly in their path, persuading the Allies to embark on an amphibious assault behind the line at Anzio. Operation Shingle, as the assault was code-named, was nothing short of a disaster. Although an attack on the Gustav Line at Monte Cassino, a key, hilltop position, diverted some of Kesselring's forces, the Allies failed to push inland from Anzio after an almost unopposed landing on January 22, 1944. For the next four months, the American and British forces were subjected to intense bombardment and attack.

A British officer walks toward the ruins of the village of Monte Cassino. The remains of a white-walled monastery can just be made out on top of one of the mountains above the town. A key part of the German defenses, the monastery was pulverized by Allied bombers. It was finally captured on May 17–18, 1944.

From Rome to Bologna

On the Gustav Line, a renewed Allied offensive in the spring was exploited by Polish forces who stormed Monte Cassino. The monastery on Monte Cassino had been virtually destroyed by Allied bombing before the assault. This attack came as part of a general aassault along the Gustav Line that began on May 11. The breakthrough at Cassino allowed Clark to advance on Rome. Rome fell on June 4, and the Germans once again built a defensive position, the Gothic Line, as their troops were diverted to northern France to oppose the Allied D-Day landings.

When the winter of 1944 arrived, there was a lull in operations. D-Day had shifted the focus of Allied and German strategy. In December Italian forces loyal to Mussolini made a surprise attack on the Allies, but this was largely ineffective.

In the spring of 1945 U.S. and British divisions launched a final attack on the Gothic Line. Massive aerial bombardment of the German forward divisions and their reinforcements had weakened their defenses, and they crumbled in the face of the advance. Bologna was liberated on April 21. Allied aircraft systematically destroyed bridges in northern Italy, denying the Germans any possibility of retreat.

The German surrender on May 2, 1945, brought to an end the bitterly contested and costly Italian campaign. Mussolini's body had been hanging on public display in Milan for nearly a week. He had been captured on the shore of Lake Como by partisans while trying to escape and had been executed. One of the major leaders of the Axis alliance was no more.

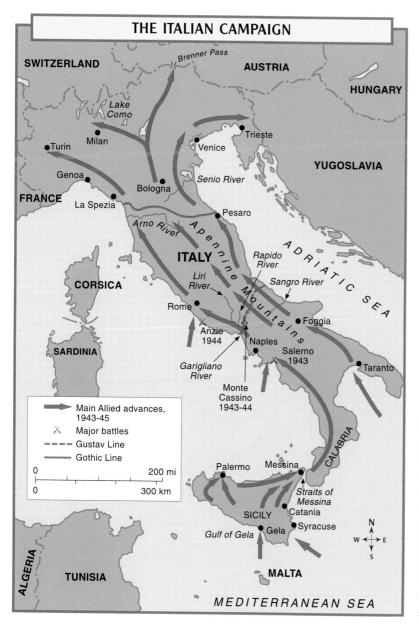

THE ITALIAN CAMPAIGN

SWITZERLAND

Brenner Pass

AUSTRIA

HUNGARY

Lake Como

Turin

Milan

Venice

Trieste

YUGOSLAVIA

Genoa

Bologna

Senio River

FRANCE

La Spezia

Pesaro

Arno River

Apennine Mountains

ITALY

ADRIATIC SEA

Rapido River

CORSICA

Liri River

Sangro River

Rome

Foggia

Anzio 1944

Naples

SARDINIA

Salerno 1943

Garigliano River

Taranto

Monte Cassino 1943-44

Main Allied advances, 1943-45

Major battles

Gustav Line

Gothic Line

0   200 mi

0   300 km

CALABRIA

Palermo

Messina

Straits of Messina

Catania

SICILY

Gulf of Gela

Gela

Syracuse

N W E S

ALGERIA

TUNISIA

MALTA

MEDITERRANEAN SEA

When the Allies invaded the Italian mainland in the late summer of 1943, they faced two problems. First, the terrain favored the German defenders. Apart from narrow strips along the west and east coasts, Italy is very mountainous. The way forward was also blocked by a series of rivers running across the line of advance, Second, the Germans were highly skilled veterans and commanded by an outstanding general, Albert von Kesselring.

39

THE SOVIET UNION STRIKES BACK

The fighting during the winter of 1942–43 was a decisive turning point in the war on the Eastern Front. The successful defense of Stalingrad by the Red Army gave the Allies their first indication that the forces of the Third Reich could be defeated on a large scale. By the summer months of 1943, the vast resources of the Soviet Union were turning the tide of the battle against Germany. After a massive battle at Kursk in July, the last major German offensive on the Eastern Front was defeated.

The Soviet counterattack at Stalingrad dealt a stunning blow to the Germans. At the start of February 1943, with the German forces hopelessly trapped in Stalingrad, Soviet armies were also threatening General Erich von Manstein's northern flank around Kharkov, a vital rail depot. Hitler ordered the city to be held and was furious when the armored division deployed to hold Kharkov abandoned it on the 15th.

Hitler immediately ordered Manstein to recapture the city. Given the fact that his army group had been forced to retreat hastily from the Caucasus across the Black Sea to the Crimean peninsula in the face of the Soviet offensive, it is remarkable that Manstein could even consider fighting back. However, he had succeeded in luring the Soviet forces some 425 miles (700 km) west of Stalingrad in a short space of time to the Dnieper River.

German troops advance through the burning suburbs of Kharkov during the fighting in the winter of 1943. The Russians captured the city in February but were thrown out by a German offensive in the following March.

ERICH VON MANSTEIN

Erich von Manstein was without doubt the greatest German commander of World War II, and many military historians consider him to be the most outstanding general of the whole war. Like many senior officers of the period, he had seen action in World War I.

After World War I Manstein served in staff and administrative posts in the German army. In 1936 he became the deputy to General Ludwig Beck, chief of the German General Staff. Manstein's military skills were first revealed during the invasion of Poland in 1939, and he played a key role in organizing the German blitzkrieg against France in 1940.

However, it was on the Eastern Front that Manstein displayed the whole range of his talents. His forces played a distinguished role in the invasion of the Soviet Union in 1941, and his capture of Kharkov in March 1943 prevented a German collapse on the Eastern Front. He also played a leading role in the Battle of Kursk in the following July.

Unlike many other German generals, Manstein was not afraid to disagree with Hitler on military matters. He was relieved of his command in March 1944 after a quarrel with Hitler.

German general Erich von Manstein (right) watches the progress of his forces during the Battle of Kursk in July 1943.

The sheer size of the Soviet forces, the speed of their advance, and their poor organization had thrown their own supply system into chaos. Soviet tactics paid little attention to the needs of supply, but atrocious winter weather and the German practice of changing wide-gauge Russian railroad lines to a narrower European gauge was a considerable hindrance. Despite the fact

Between February 1943 and January 1944, the Red Army launched a number of attacks on the Germans. The Germans also launched two major offensives themselves. The first, fought between February and March 1943, was able to retake Kharkov. The second, against Kursk in July 1943, was a disaster. The Red Army defeated the German advance and inflicted severe casualties on their enemy.

THE RUSSIAN FRONT, 1943-44

- - - · - Front line, February 1943
- - - - Front line, January 1944
——— Hagen Line
✕ Major battles

0 — 400 mi
0 — 600 km

FINLAND
Lake Ladoga
Leningrad 1941-43
Riga
Moscow
RUSSIA
Volga River
EAST PRUSSIA
Orel
Kursk 1943
Smolensk
Voronezh
Minsk
Prokhorovka
Don River
Stalingrad
Kiev 1943
Kharkov 1943
Donets River
POLAND
Dnieper River
Zhitomir 1943
Rostov
Lvov
CAUCASUS
HUNGARY
Odessa
CRIMEA
KERCH STRAIT
ROMANIA
BLACK SEA
N / S / W / E

that Kharkov was a major railroad junction, all Soviet supplies had to be trucked across hundreds of miles of open country. This put the Soviet forces commanded by General Nikolai Vatutin in a weakened position.

Kharkov recaptured

For the spring offensive demanded by Hitler, Manstein planned to drive the Russians back across the Donets River. Manstein's armies would then attack and recapture Kharkov. Manstein's forces had nearly a seven to one superiority in tanks, and the Luftwaffe outnumbered the Soviet Union's Red Air Force by three to one. The Germans attacked on February 20. The Soviet forces, low on fuel and supplies, were rapidly driven back. Vatutin tried to halt the retreat, but the German tanks were rolling with a seemingly unstoppable force.

Kharkov fell on March 15, but it was the last time that the city would be in German hands. Kharkov was a major disaster for the Red Army. Vatutin's forces had been pushed back across the Donets River by the ferocity of the German attack. Its units had suffered over 72,000 casualties and had 600 tanks destroyed. Yet the Red Army had no problems with reinforcements, and seemingly could afford to lose legions of tanks and men. The Germans could not afford to lose men and equipment on such a scale.

The lull in fighting during the late spring of 1943 came at a vital time for the Germans, who desperately needed time to rest and reequip. With this in mind, the high command planned no major offensive for the summer. The spring thaw had, as expected, turned the landscape into a swamp, conditions in which the German tanks could not operate. This gave the field workshops time to catch up with their backlog of repairs, but there were fewer tanks available than at any other time in the conflict.

In order to straighten the line the Germans planned a limited offensive to take the town of Kursk, where the front line had a noteworthy bulge, by a pincer movement. Delays in the start of the offensive allowed the Soviet forces under General Georgi Zhukov considerable time to prepare defensive works around Kursk. To the Germans, the attack on Kursk seemed an opportunity to destroy substantial Soviet forces, despite the fears of some German generals that the operation was far too ambitious.

The Battle of Kursk

The German attack, Operation Citadel, was planned for July 5, with General Walther Model's Ninth Army driving south from Orel in a two-pronged attack. On the southern flank of the Kursk position Manstein planned to drive northeast to cut off the Soviet retreat. Warned by a deserter of the exact time of the German attack, the Red Army unleashed their artillery on Model's men. The German advance rapidly got bogged down among densely sown minefields. The attack was stopped dead in its tracks only 12 miles (19 km) from its starting point. Many of the new German tanks broke down. Model had lost half of his tanks by July 12.

German tanks move forward toward the Red Army's positions around Kursk shortly before the opening of their attack on July 5, 1943. Note that the tanks have been fitted with extra armor around their turrets and on the sides to protect their tracks and wheels.

In the south the larger number of German tanks seemed an advantage, but heavily wooded countryside gave the Red Army's antitank gunners superb cover to destroy tanks at close range. The Germans were unable to break through until July 8. Two days later the German forces had smashed through the Soviet line almost to the village of Prokhorovka. On July 11, German units crossed a small river, the last line of defense in front of Kursk.

At this point the Red Army launched a counterattack with 850 tanks. The 700 German tanks that opposed them were compressed into a small area, and any advantage the Germans had previously possessed due to the greater range of their guns was lost. The Soviet tank crews, many women among them, fought with a tenacity and heroism that after eight hours of battle had seriously weakened the German tank units.

On July 15, Soviet forces attacked toward Orel from their position on the northern flank of the Kursk battlefield. The other half of the Red Army's counterattack was delayed by the need to regroup, but on August 3 an attack opened a 40-mile (64-km) gap in the German defensive line. Soviet units poured through this gap and headed for Kharkov On August 20, Hitler made a

ZHUKOV AND THE BATTLE OF KURSK

The commander of the Red Army at the Battle of Kursk was Georgi Zhukov, the general who would lead the Red Army into Berlin in 1945. In 1943 Zhukov knew that the Germans intended to attack Kursk and set about turning the area around the town into a fortress.

Kursk was protected by three lines of defenses. Each line was made up of densely sown minefields, thick belts of barbed wire, trenches to shelter Red Army troops, and camouflaged positions containing antitank guns and artillery.

Zhukov's plan for the forthcoming battle was simple. He intended to blunt the first German attacks, which would have to cut through his three bands of defenses before they could reach Kursk. Zhukov believed that the fighting to break through his defenses would reduce the strength of the Germans.

Zhukov also kept a number of armored units in reserve. If the weakened Germans did manage to cut through toward Kursk, he would unleash his own tanks against the enemy. Soviet air units were used to defeat the German air force and support Soviet ground units.

Zhukov's plan worked. Germany had 70,000 men killed and wounded, 3,000 tanks and 1,000 cannon destroyed or abandoned, and 1,400 aircraft shot down.

rare decision, to retreat from Kharkov. In any case, by August 18, the German retreat was widespread. In the following week, Soviet forces crossed the upper reaches of the Donets River, while other troops drove far enough westward to threaten to crush a German army in the south. Between September 3 and October 9, nearly 250,000 German troops were evacuated from the Caucasus into the Crimea. The defeat of the German attack on Kursk was decisive—it was the last major German attack on the Eastern Front—and marked the beginning of the advance that would take the Red Army to Berlin, the German capital.

Headlong German retreat

While Model was being forced back toward the city of Orel north of Kursk, other Red Army forces attacked elsewhere. The Hagen Line, a German defensive position near Kursk, was attacked on August 29. Weakly defended by the 300 or so tanks, the Germans were driven back, at some points over 150 miles (240 km). In the south German troops were forced to retreat as far as the Dnieper River, where their engineers set to work constructing elaborate defensive works on the river's western banks. Yet, on September 24, the Red Army established small toe-holds on the western bank of the river.

Thousands of Soviet troops poured across the river, followed by armored support once pontoon bridges had been erected. By mid-October, the Germans had been pushed back along a 440-mile (708-km) front. On November 3 Soviet forces assaulted Kiev, but encountered strong resistance from the German defenders, who held the city until the 12th. However, German forces in the Crimean peninsula were cut off, with little hope of escape.

The intense period of fighting on the Eastern Front in 1943 came to a temporary end as freezing weather halted operations. While the battered Germans paused to draw breath and regroup, the Red Army was steeling itself for the final onslaught that would drive the invaders from the Soviet Union.

Red Army horse-drawn artillery moves forward protected by ground-attack aircraft after the Red Army's victory at Kursk in June 1943. The ground-attack aircraft carried an array of rockets, cannon, and bombs. They were well able to deal with any German tank that they could spot while flying low over a battlefield.

THE STRUGGLE FOR THE SKIES

At the outbreak of World War II, few recognized the importance of aircraft in modern warfare. The aircraft available were not greatly different from many that had seen service over the previous 20 years. By the end of the war, however, aircraft were flying higher, faster, and for longer than ever before. Some pilots were even flying the first jet-powered fighters. Aircraft were performing more roles than ever and had a decisive impact on the ground war. Long-range Allied bombers were also waging a campaign to bring Germany and Japan to their knees.

Four P-51 Mustang fighters of the United States Army Air Force patrol the skies over Europe. The Mustang was one of the best aircraft of the war. One of its greatest assets was its range (the distance it could fly from its base). It could protect bombers attacking targets in the heart of Germany.

Of all the European nations that entered the war in 1939 only Germany was adequately prepared to fight a large-scale air war. Though forbidden to do so under conditions of the Treaty of Versailles, the Luftwaffe (Germany's air force) had built up its strength during the mid-1930s and possessed the most powerful fleet of aircraft in the world by 1939.

Between the wars, the British Royal Air Force's (RAF) senior command clung to the belief that strategic bombing would form the key to any future air war and equipped itself with bombers. Other vital areas of military aviation were ignored, and naval aviation was not developed. By 1939, most of the RAF's equipment was old, and there was a desperate shortage of experienced pilots. It was only due to the energies of Sir Hugh Dowding, head of the RAF's Fighter Command, and Minister for Production Max

Beaverbrook that the RAF's strength was at a level where it could stand a chance of defeating the Luftwaffe by July 1940.

In America, the United States Army Air Force (USAAF) underwent a crash program after the outbreak of war in Europe to build up its strength and train an adequate number of pilots. By December 1941, it had 25,000 personnel and 4,000 aircraft, including the only four-engined strategic bomber in the world. These long-range bombers, operating from airfields in eastern England, played a decisive role in the outcome of the war by launching mass daylight raids on Nazi-occupied Europe from 1943 onward.

Fighter operations

The range of roles that fighter aircraft, such as the RAF's Spitfire, Germany's Messerschmitt Bf 109, America's P-51 Mustang, and Japan's Mitsubishi A6M Zero, were adapted to was quite remarkable. The RAF was the first air force to introduce a revolutionary low-wing monoplane (single-wing) fighter in 1937, but failed to take advantage of this early lead. The Luftwaffe responded with the Bf 109. Over the skies of southern England the Bf 109 fought the Spitfire during the Battle of Britain in the summer of 1940, but came off worse.

The use of long-range fighter escorts, such as the Mustang and Republican Thunderbolt, to protect USAAF bombers operating over Europe was a truly significant development in the air war. Previously bombers had to attack targets deep in Europe without fighter protection. Allied losses to German fighters were huge, but with the deployment of escorts, the losses fell dramatically. Germany tried to counter the growing Allied superiority in fighters and bombers with increasingly sophisticated aircraft such as the Messerschmitt Me 262 jet fighter, but the production lines

RADAR

Radar has gone largely unrecognized as one of the truly decisive weapons of World War II. Although research and development work was carried out in Britain, Germany, Japan, the United States, and the Soviet Union during the interwar years, by 1939 the British led the field. As far back as 1937 construction began on a land-based early warning system around the English coast. During the Battle of Britain this system gave the British a vital advantage by enabling them to predict the strength, direction, and height of attacking German aircraft.

In 1940 a crude form of airborne radar became available to the British. This was used with some success by night-fighter units to find enemy bomber formations in the dark during the winter of 1940–41.

A vital breakthrough in the Battle of the Atlantic came when Allied maritime patrol aircraft began to use radar in their hunts for surfaced U-boats. During the course of the war no other new technology advanced so far or had such a profound impact on the outcome of the war as did radar.

could not meet demand in the face of incessant bombing. In the last months of the war, Allied forces enjoyed almost complete air superiority over Germany.

Bombing operations

World War II saw an enormous growth in strategic air power, the ability of aircraft to strike deep inside enemy territory against factories, vital rail and road junctions, and other economic targets. The interwar years had been a time of serious, and occasionally bitter, debate on the future role of aircraft. Some believed that there was a need for bombers that could deliver heavy bomb loads over long distances, effectively destroying an enemy's ability to fight. Others spoke in favor of fast, medium bombers and dive-bombers to directly support ground forces.

Three of the RAF's long-range Lancaster bombers pictured on a training mission. The Lancaster made up the bulk of the RAF's bomber force during the war. It was a well-engineered and reliable aircraft.

The USAAF was farsighted in its purchase of the B-17 Flying Fortress bombers in the late 1930s. Although the RAF had concentrated on strategic bombing during the interwar years, it could field only 350 bombers in 1939. By 1944, the height of the offensive against the Axis powers, the USAAF and RAF had around 10,000 bombers in service.

Early bombing operations, particularly by the British, were carried out during daylight hours at long-range. Experience quickly showed the RAF that such tactics, without fighter escorts, were suicidal. Losses grew to dangerously high levels and the British switched to night raids on enemy targets, believing that the cover of darkness would reduce losses to acceptable levels.

All air forces had entered the war with a policy of attacking military targets only, although this policy was soon abandoned. The failure of the RAF to accurately bomb individual targets at night with pinpoint accuracy led to the adoption of "area bombing" by the head of Bomber Command, Sir Arthur Harris.

When the considerable bomber resources of the United States became available for use in Europe, a joint bombing program began. From 1943 night offensives were conducted against the industrial cities of the Ruhr, Hamburg, and Berlin by the RAF, while U.S. bombers, protected by long-range versions of the Mustang fighter from 1944, continued mass daylight raids.

Germany never really developed a long-range bomber force and apart from mass raids on British cities in 1940 never launched a strategic bomber offensive. However, during 1944–45, Germany used the world's first long-range rockets, code-named V-1 and V-2, to hit London. They did not influence the outcome of the war, but frightened civilians and showed that such rockets could play a role in modern warfare.

Japan was subjected to Allied strategic bombing from late 1944, after American forces had captured islands within bombing range of the Japanese heartland. Attacks devastated many of the major Japanese cities, but the enormous destruction and loss of life did not force the Japanese to surrender or end their will to fight on. It was only the dropping of the first atomic bombs on the Japanese cities of Hiroshima and Nagasaki in August 1945 that ended the war in the Pacific—and World War II.

WOMEN AT WAR

With the exception of the Soviet Union, where women did fight in both ground and air units, the rival countries in World War II did not use females in combat roles. However, women did serve near the front as nurses in field hospitals or in administrative positions with most armies. British women volunteered to serve in organizations such as the Wrens (Women's Royal Naval Service). Their jobs were vital because they provided the backup that allowed commanders to use their troops to the best advantage.

Women also worked in factories, making weapons and ammunition, as well as armored vehicles and aircraft. Others were or became pilots, and flew aircraft from where they were built to the units that would actually use them. In America, Women's Airforce Service Pilots (WASPs) transported all types of military planes 60 million miles (96 million km) in noncombat areas for the USAAF.

The one exception to using women in war-related industries was Germany, where the Nazis believed that they should carry out more traditional roles, such as looking after the home and children. Some German women did work in administrative jobs for the German armed forces, but the majority were not allowed to make the weapons that Germany needed to fight World War II.

An American factory worker examines artillery shell cases for the quality of their finish.

THE PACIFIC TIDE TURNS

By the beginning of 1943 the United States and its Allied forces were firmly on the offensive across the Pacific. In a series of large-scale land and sea battles, these forces regained the initiative in this theater of operations. They forced the Japanese to fight increasingly defensive battles to defend the territory they had taken in the first months of the war, each one ever closer to Japan. By the end of 1944 the Japanese fleet had been devastated by U.S. carrier-based air power and the route back to the Philippines for the forces led by General Douglas MacArthur was wide open.

Throughout the fall of 1942 Japanese supply convoys, nicknamed by American troops the "Tokyo Express," continued to land reinforcements to attack the U.S. air base at Henderson Field on Guadalcanal (see page 35). These troops were used in a series of almost round-the-clock attacks against the island's U.S. Marine defenders, who showed extreme courage in crushing the Japanese. In the seas surrounding Guadalcanal and other of the Solomon Islands, the U.S. and Japanese navies fought seven major battles to secure control of the waters off the islands.

Battle for the Solomons

On land, the Japanese forces were crippled by supply problems and were forced to retreat to the northern tip of Guadalcanal by repeated American offensives. Due to their mounting losses, the

U.S. nurses arrive on New Guinea to establish a field hospital to treat the sick and wounded American and Australian troops who had been fighting to evict the Japanese from the island.

Japanese began to withdraw from Guadalcanal on December 31, 1942, and by February 9, 1943, the island was firmly in American hands. The final capture of Guadalcanal brought immense advantages to the Allies. Australia and New Zealand were safe from Japanese attack, and Allied forces now stood ready to launch further counterattacks in the southwest Pacific.

On New Guinea, Australian troops made contact with Japanese forces advancing across the island's Owen Stanley Mountains toward Port Moresby in August 1942. A month of savage combat along the narrow Kokoda Trail, the only practical route through the mountains, forced the Japanese to take up defensive positions. These were captured in January 1943, but only after some of the bitterest combat of the war. Fierce fighting continued elsewhere through the spring.

The fight for New Georgia

In March, a Japanese convoy taking troops to New Guinea was hammered by U.S. aircraft in the Battle of the Bismarck Sea. This action effectively cut off the Japanese forces on New Guinea and led the Allies to develop further strategic aims. They planned a two-pronged attack, code-named Operation Cartwheel. Admiral William Halsey's U.S. Third Fleet moved through the Solomons in July, with the aim of capturing Rabaul on New Britain.

Landings on the New Georgia island group in the eastern Solomons were coordinated with assaults on New Guinea to the west by forces under MacArthur. The rapid advance of MacArthur's troops along the coast of New Guinea was achieved by a series of leapfrogging amphibious assaults, ending in the capture of the vital port of Finschhafen on October 2.

DOUGLAS MACARTHUR

General Douglas MacArthur was one of the greatest commanders of his generation. His amphibious campaigns in the Pacific are widely regarded as great examples of the military strategist's art. However, MacArthur was also a controversial figure, one often at odds with other generals and senior U.S. politicians.

MacArthur was born into an army family in Little Rock, Arkansas, on January 26, 1880. He served in the Philippines during 1903, the year he became a junior officer. He rose rapidly through the ranks and was commander of a division by the end of World War I. Further tours of the Philippines were followed by his appointment as the U.S. Army's chief of staff in November 1930. MacArthur was in charge of the spirited but unsuccessful defense of the Philippines against the Japanese in the early months of World War II. After evacuating to Australia, he masterminded the U.S. counterattack in the southwest Pacific, ending in the liberation of the Philippines in 1944–45.

During the Korean War (1951–53) MacArthur was the commander of the United Nations forces defending South Korea from attack by North Korea until his replacement in April 1951 after he had disagreed over the conduct of the war with President Harry S Truman.

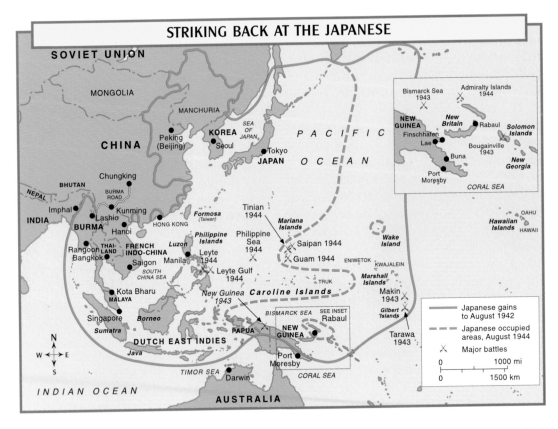

STRIKING BACK AT THE JAPANESE

The war in the Pacific as fought between August 1942 to August 1944. By 1943, Allied forces began to recapture the territories and islands captured by the Japanese in the first months of the war. Each hard-fought victory brought the Allies ever closer to Japan itself.

On Christmas Day, 1943, the battle-weary troops who had fought so hard to secure the northeastern parts of New Guinea had a magnificent demonstration of their success. A huge American invasion fleet passed them and began to land the U.S. First Marine Division on New Britain, MacArthur's next target.

From the Solomons to the Marianas

Halsey's forces were equally successful. Battling through the central Solomons during the summer, they forced the Japanese to withdraw to Bougainville, the most northerly of the Solomons. An assault by U.S. Marines began on November 1, with the aim of capturing the harbors and airfields that had supplied Japanese troops on Guadalcanal. Japanese strength on the islands was estimated at 40,000 men, but their attacks were successfully beaten off. The U.S. success was in part due to the use of Navajo radio operators. These Native Americans devised a secret code based on their own language, which the Japanese never cracked, thereby allowing the safe transmission of orders and messages. Isolated groups of Japanese continued to fight until 1945, but the building of a U.S. airfield on the island was largely unopposed, and this allowed the Americans to attack Rabaul on New Britain.

In the Central Pacific an ambitious assault was prepared by Admiral Chester Nimitz in the summer of 1943. With the return of Halsey's fleet to his command after its successes in the Solomons, Nimitz had considerable forces to attack the heart of the Japanese perimeter. On November 20, 1943, U.S. amphibious forces landed on Makin and Tarawa in the Gilbert Islands. Both were captured after a few days, although there was especially hard fighting on Tarawa. Back in the southwest Pacific, MacArthur captured the Admiralty Islands with a daring operation that began in February 1944.

Under the threat from the converging U.S. drives from the southwest and Central Pacific, the Japanese fleet sailed to challenge Nimitz's forces around the Mariana Islands, and suffered defeat at the Battle of the Philippine Sea in June. The battle was known to the Americans as the "Great Marianas Turkey Shoot." Three Japanese carriers and over 400 aircraft were destroyed.

The Battle of the Philippine Sea brought an end to any real hopes the Japanese navy had of stemming the U.S. advance. With naval units covering the amphibious troops, the U.S. assault on Guam, one of the main Mariana Islands, began on July 21. Japanese resistance on Guam and the nearby islands of Saipan and Tinian was ended by mid-August. The capture of the Marianas was vital to the bombing offensive against Japan. The islands were within flying range of Japan. Until the islands' capture the U.S. had been planning to bomb Japan from bases in China.

MacArthur's return to the Philippines

With the battles for the southwest and Central Pacific islands won, the U.S. generals and admirals could now focus on the Philippines, and then turn to Japan itself. While Admiral Ernest J. King, commander-in-chief of the U.S. Fleet and Chief of Naval Operations, favored a direct assault on Formosa (now Taiwan) after the victories in the Marianas and on New Guinea,

U.S. Marines move off the beach at Tarawa to attack Japanese positions in the island's interior. Tarawa, in November 1943, was one of the Marines' most costly battles of the whole war. The Japanese were protected by trenches and hidden positions. The fighting lasted from the 20th to the 24th. Only 100 Japanese were taken alive out of a garrison of 4,700. The Marines had 985 men killed and 2,193 wounded.

JAPANESE AMERICANS AT WAR

An army instructor teaches a Japanese American the correct drill for using a mortar.

The Japanese attack on Pearl Harbor in December 1941 led to a considerable public and government backlash against people of Japanese descent who lived in the U.S. At the time there were 112,000 Japanese on the West Coast, including 72,000 Nisei (second generation, or U.S. born Japanese) and 40,000 Issei (first, or immigrant generation). It was thought that they would side with Japan rather than fight for the United States.

On February 19, 1942, a time when fears of a Japanese invasion were still high, an executive order was given to the secretary of state to move the Japanese Americans away from the coast to ten camps in the interior. Despite moves to prevent the relocation, the secretary of state's decision was upheld by the Supreme Court. The Supreme Court confirmed the deportation despite the Federal Bureau of Investigation having already rounded up all those it considered a risk.

Japanese Americans were eventually allowed to fight for the U.S. The 100th Infantry Battalion became one of the most decorated U.S. Army units of the whole war.

MacArthur argued successfully for an attack on Luzon in the Philippines. The U.S. forces began the campaign by attacking the Philippine island of Leyte.

General Walter Krueger's U.S. Sixth Army made a highly successful landing on Leyte that began on October 22, but this was largely overshadowed by the naval battle for Leyte Gulf, which remains the largest naval engagement in history. The Japanese were fully aware that the establishment of U.S. air bases on Leyte, just 300 miles (480 km) to the southeast of Luzon, would force them to abandon the Philippines. The Japanese knew that without the Philippines their defensive perimeter protecting Japan itself would be in tatters. The Philippines were defended by some

350,000 Japanese troops. The Japanese had already planned a last-ditch operation, code-named Sho-Go, just in case the Americans made any attempt to recapture the Philippines.

As part of this operation the Japanese planned to draw Halsey's Third Fleet into a naval action, crush it, and save the Philippines. The plan called for the use of every remaining major Japanese warship. These were split between two strike forces, while a third force consisting of Japan's four remaining large carriers, was to be used as bait to draw the U.S. forces into a trap.

The Japanese plan was complicated but at one stage came very close to success. A series of battles were fought in the waters around the Philippines between October 23rd and 25th. By the time the Japanese retreated, their navy had virtually ceased to exist as a fighting force. Four aircraft carriers, three battleships and 22 other warships had been sent to the bottom, and most of those still afloat had been damaged. Some 500 Japanese aircraft had been destroyed and 10,500 sailors and airmen killed. U.S. losses were comparatively light: three small carriers, three destroyers, and 200 aircraft. U.S. casualties were some 2,800 men killed and 1,000 wounded.

A Japanese suicide plane explodes after crashing on the deck of the U.S. Navy's carrier Intrepid *on November 24, 1944.*

The first kamikaze attacks

The surviving Japanese ships could no longer provide any effective opposition to the U.S. Pacific Fleet or guard the seas around Japan, where U.S. submarines were sinking Japanese supply ships at will. In desperation, the Japanese began to form kamikaze (divine wind) units (see page 73) to halt the advance of the U.S. forces. These were suicide units of volunteer pilots, who had pledged to crash their aircraft into American ships. They could not halt the landings on Luzon, however.

The landings began on January 9, 1945. There was desperate fighting for Manila, the Philippine capital, which was captured by U.S. forces in March. Despite the loss of Manila, the Japanese fought on, only delaying the inevitable. The last survivors of the Japanese garrison surrendered on August 15.

THE BATTLE FOR BURMA

At the outbreak of World War II Burma was part of Britain's extensive colonial empire in the Far East. Burma was a likely target for the Japanese, particularly as the capture of Burma would allow the Japanese to attack India, Britain's most important colony. In January 1942 the Japanese attacked Burma from Thailand, which they had recently captured, to halt the flow of supplies from India to China along the Burma Road. This invasion was the first act in a campaign that was one of the bitterest in World War II.

The Japanese in Burma were opposed by a small British-led army supported by Chinese forces. Air attacks on the Burmese capital, Rangoon, began on December 23. In the following months the Japanese advanced north, taking Rangoon on March 7. Two Chinese armies under U.S. General Joseph Stilwell and the U.S. volunteer pilots of General Claire Chennault's "Flying Tigers" could do little to halt the Japanese advance. By April 29, Lashio, a key town on the Burma Road, was in Japanese hands. The British made a long retreat back to India.

India under threat

British attempts to attack Burma from Assam in northern India in November 1942 were hampered by torrential rain and a lack of supplies. At this stage of the war Burma was a low priority compared to the European and Mediterranean theaters. A limited offensive on Burma's northwest Arakan coast began in December but was a disaster. For the next two years the Allies satisfied themselves with hit-and-run raids behind Japanese lines.

In March 1944 the Japanese launched an invasion of India by striking at the towns of Kohima and Imphal. The British under General William Slim met the attack head on. Both Imphal and Kohima were besieged by the Japanese but the British hung on. The Japanese, who suffered very high casualties, began to retreat in July.

Stubborn Japanese defense hampered the Allied operation to recapture Burma, but by November 1944 the British had

British and Indian troops open fire on a Japanese position as they fight their way into Mandalay, Burma's second city, in March 1945.

crossed the Chindwin River and were near Mandalay. The capture of Wanting by Chinese forces in January 1945 permitted the reopening of the Burma Road. On May 1, as British forces advanced on Rangoon, an amphibious assault was launched to retake the capital. Although there were later clashes between Allied and Japanese forces, Burma was liberated.

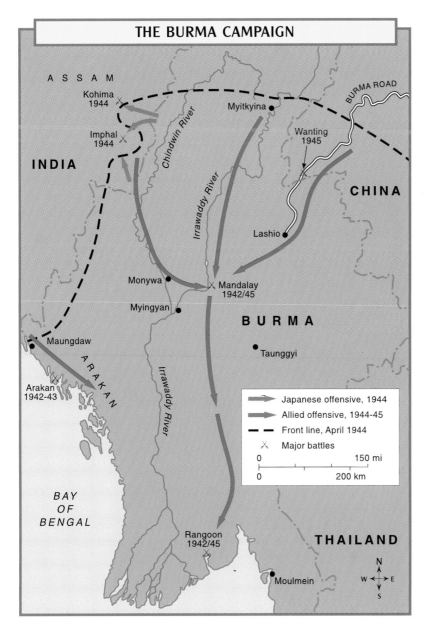

THE BURMA CAMPAIGN

ASSAM

Kohima
1944

Myitkyina

BURMA ROAD

Imphal
1944

INDIA

Chindwin River

Wanting
1945

CHINA

Irrawaddy River

Lashio

Monywa

Mandalay
1942/45

Myingyan

BURMA

Maungdaw

Taunggyi

ARAKAN

Arakan
1942-43

Irrawaddy River

	Japanese offensive, 1944
	Allied offensive, 1944-45
- - -	Front line, April 1944
✕	Major battles

0   150 mi

0   200 km

BAY
OF
BENGAL

Rangoon
1942/45

THAILAND

Moulmein

N
W ← → E
S

The war in Burma involved some of the worst conditions encountered anywhere in World War II. Difficult terrain, often awful weather, and numerous diseases conspired against the troops of both sides.

OPENING THE SECOND FRONT

Plans for the cross-Channel invasion of France had been drawn up by the British as early as September 1941, but serious discussion of an invasion began in earnest after the United States entered the war in December. By the end of May 1944, the complex invasion plans were set to become reality. Southern England was an armed camp, full of the troops and equipment needed to carry out the mission. The largest amphibious operation in warfare, code-named Overlord, was ready to strike across the English Channel.

The men who planned the Allied invasion of Europe pose for a photograph. They include General Dwight D. Eisenhower (front row, center) and General Bernard Montgomery (front row, right).

Both the Allied invasion of northwestern Africa in 1942 and the invasion of Italy in 1943 delayed the opening of the campaign in northern Europe. These campaigns, although important, were only secondary. France, just a few miles across the English Channel, was the decisive battleground in Nazi-occupied Western Europe. Hitler had ordered the creation of a vast defensive line to protect the coast, but the Allies had steadily built up their own forces in Britain. If Hitler could be forced to fight on the Eastern Front and in Western Europe at the same time, it was unlikely that Nazi Germany could survive.

Planning the invasion

The plan for the Normandy invasion was accepted among the Allies by the end of 1943 and planning eventually passed to the newly appointed Supreme Allied Commander, General Dwight D. Eisenhower. A code-name, Overlord, was chosen, and British General Bernard Montgomery was selected to be the operation's overall commander. The Allies had many things to consider—where to land in France, how to organize the invasion, and how to fool the Germans.

Elaborate deception plans were put in place, which depended heavily on the use of radio. Fake radio transmissions suggested that General George Patton's U.S. First Army Group, a unit that did not in fact exist, was to invade across the narrowest part of

DWIGHT D. EISENHOWER

General Dwight D. Eisenhower, the supreme commander of all the Allied forces involved in D-Day and the liberation of Western Europe, had two great qualities. First, he had immense organizational skills, which were essential in planning an operation as complex as D-Day. Second, he was a thoughtful and sincere diplomat, which allowed him to resolve any arguments between the American and British generals under his command.

Eisenhower was born in Texas and served in World War I. Before World War II, he attended various military colleges and was promoted to the rank of brigadier general shortly before America's entry into World War II in December 1941. His first major operation was as commander of the Allied landings in North Africa in November 1943.

After overseeing the Allied invasions of Sicily and the Italian mainland in 1943, he traveled to England, where he was made Supreme Commander of the Allied Expeditionary Force, and was charged with planning the invasion of France. Eisenhower coordinated all of the Allied forces until the end of the war.

After the war, he continued to hold senior military posts until 1952, when he was elected U.S. president for the first of the two terms he served.

the English Channel, from Dover to Calais. In reality a massive invasion force was gathering in southern England for a projected assault on five beaches in Normandy, part of northern France, well away from Calais and its defenses. The force, consisting of nearly three million men, was to be supported by a massive air and sea bombardment. Control of the air was a vital part of the Allied plan, and Eisenhower decided to delay the invasion by one month to further reduce the Luftwaffe through Allied air attacks.

German generals disagree

The deception plan proved effective and led to serious worries in the German command. The commander of the German forces defending France against invasion was the veteran Field Marshal Gerd von Rundstedt. He believed there was little hope of containing the Allies on the beaches and favored maintaining a strong reserve to launch counterattacks.

Field Marshal Erwin Rommel, commander of a number of German armies in northwestern France and the Low Countries, believed Allied air power would destroy Rundstedt's forces before they could get to grips with the invaders, and he backed a

U.S. troops and their vehicles land on Omaha Beach, D-Day, June 6, 1944. Omaha was a tough nut to crack.. The assault forces, led by the First Infantry Division, suffered heavy casualties before they could move off the beach and head farther inland.

plan to fight on the beaches. Rommel was the only German general who had experienced Allied air power at first hand, during his battles in North Africa. Hitler imposed a plan that satisfied neither general. Significantly, all three men expected the attack to come around Calais, and German units were concentrated there.

Supported by air forces that contained 13,000 U.S. aircraft alone, a naval force set course across the English Channel before dawn of June 6, 1944. Airborne forces were dropped behind the beaches. Shortly afterward, British and Canadian troops stormed ashore on three beaches, code-named Gold, Juno, and Sword. These landings met some, occasionally heavy, resistance.

The Allied breakout from Normandy

Farther west, the American landings on one beach, code-named Omaha, were hindered by heavy surf, steep cliffs, and much more stubborn German resistance. Losses were heavy, but the U.S. troops held on. At Utah, the other American landing beach, troops met little resistance. Hitler was slow to react, believing the Normandy landings were a trick, and he delayed moving troops from Calais. By the evening of June 6, the Allied landing troops were ashore and beachheads had been established.

Hitler's insistence on interfering in the battle for Normandy caused problems for the German generals. He refused to commit large numbers of reinforcements to the fighting despite pleas from Rommel and Rundstedt. Allied air attacks also continued to strike at the German divisions in Normandy during the weeks after the landings, and although storms in the Channel destroyed one of the the artificial concrete harbors erected to facilitate the unloading of troops and supplies at the beaches, the Allied advance inland made slow but steady progress.

American forces captured the port of Cherbourg on June 26, and by July 1, the Allies had equaled the German forces in strength. Despite nearly one million men and 177,000 vehicles opposing him, Hitler still continued to refuse to release divisions from around Calais.

General Omar Bradley's U.S. First Army made a vital break-out to Avranches on July 31 and secured the Cotentin Peninsula, but the British had to fight hard to evict the Germans from Caen,

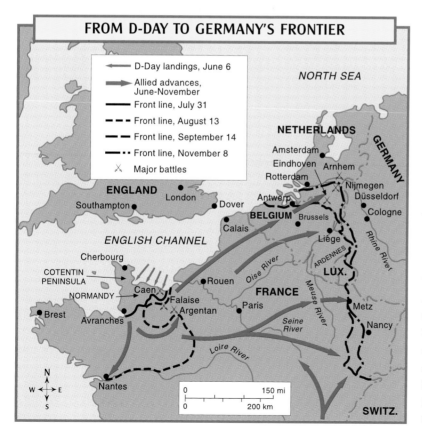

FROM D-DAY TO GERMANY'S FRONTIER

← D-Day landings, June 6

➡ Allied advances, June–November

▬ Front line, July 31

▪ ▪ ▪ Front line, August 13

▬ ▬ Front line, September 14

▬ ▪ ▪ Front line, November 8

✕ Major battles

The Allies advance from the Normandy invasion beaches in June 1944 and drive toward the German border, which was reached by the end of the year. There was hard fighting to break out of Normandy but the Allies then moved quickly across northern France as the Germans retreated back to their own frontier.

GEORGE S. PATTON

California-born George Patton was one of the few Allied generals who understood the concept of armored warfare, and despite his often blunt manner, his leadership proved inspirational and determined in many theaters of the war. After graduating from West Point in 1909, he was commissioned into a cavalry unit, and during World War I saw service on the Western Front. While in France he became the first U.S. officer to receive tank training.

During the interwar years Patton held various staff posts, but was given command of the U.S. Second Armored Division in January 1942. He was involved in planning the invasion of North Africa in November 1943 and masterminded the eastward drive of the Seventh Army through Tunisia. Later he commanded the same unit during the Sicilian campaign, but was reprimanded for accusing a shell-shocked soldier of cowardice.

Patton led the U.S. Third Army after the invasion of France in 1944. During the subsequent breakout from Normandy and the drive to eastern France, he showed strokes of military genius. He responded to the German Ardennes offensive in late 1944 with a brilliant counterattack, and crossed the Rhine River in March 1945. Patton died of his injuries after a car crash in December of that year, robbing the U.S. Army of one of its most capable leaders.

Armored warfare expert George Patton.

but the battle at Caen drew in German units that could have stopped Bradley's breakout. Finally, the sweeping advance of the U.S. armies forced the Germans to retreat. Many, however, did not escape. Trapped by the British advancing south from Caen and the Americans moving north, some 50,000 surrendered in the Falaise-Argentan area in mid-August.

On August 15, an Allied amphibious landing took place between Cannes and Toulon along the coast of southern France. The Germans, under attack from the northwest and south of

France, were forced to retreat. The Second Free French Armored Division, made up of Frenchmen, led by General Jacques Philippe Leclerc, who had escaped from the defeat of 1940, and the U.S. Fourth Infantry Division liberated Paris on August 25.

The advance through France had left the Allied supply lines overstretched, and their armies were still using the temporary harbor in Normandy as they had yet to capture a major port. This lack of supplies slowed the Allied attack and gave the Germans time to prepare their defenses. Eisenhower, the supreme commander of the Allied forces in Europe, continued the Allied advance, provoking arguments between his field commanders, Montgomery and Patton, who were both eager to see a concentration of effort behind their own attacks.

Disaster at Arnhem

Eisenhower supported Montgomery's disastrous airborne assault at Arnhem, Operation Market Garden, which was designed to capture three important bridges over the Rhine River in the Netherlands intact and speed the Allied advance into Germany. The attack began on September 17 and rapidly ran into trouble.

The defeat at Arnhem showed that, although the Germans were retreating, they were far from beaten. As the weary Allies settled down for the winter of 1944–45, the Germans were planning a massive counterattack through the Ardennes, the scene of their great breakthrough in 1940. On its success or failure would hinge the outcome of the war in Western Europe.

British paratroopers prepare to move toward the Dutch town of Arnhem after the first landings of Operation Market Garden, September 1944. American paratroopers were also involved in the attack, and were able to capture two bridges. The British at Arnhem, where a bridge crossed the Rhine River, fought against great odds but were finally defeated.

INTO THE THIRD REICH

By the winter of 1944–45, the Allies were poised to advance into Germany but bad weather, fatigue, and supply problems were forcing them to slow the pace of their advance. The Germans decided to gamble everything on one last offensive—a massive attack through the thinly defended Ardennes area in Belgium. Their objective was the port of Antwerp to the north, but before the Germans could advance on the port, they had to capture Bastogne, a vital center of communications held by U.S. troops.

Hitler still had 65 divisions with which to defend Germany's western border. Many of them were filled with old men and youngsters aged from 16 to 60. Equipment, especially fuel, was in short supply. But in the late fall of 1944 Hitler was still considering an attack that might force the Allies into a negotiated peace settlement. He correctly judged that the eastward drive by Montgomery's force and Bradley's armies had placed great strains on the Allied supply lines, which were still somewhat dependent on the remaining artificial harbor in Normandy.

British and Canadian troops had had to fight hard to clear German-occupied islands at the mouth of the Scheldt Estuary, which led to Antwerp, in October and November. With these in Allied hands ships could begin unloading supplies at Antwerp.

American troops, members of an artillery unit, man a machine gun during the early stages of the Battle of the Bulge, December 1944. The overcast weather, as seen here, caused many problems for the Allies. Their aircraft could not find enemy targets to attack. However, when the weather cleared they were able to hit the Germans hard.

The first supplies reached the port on November 28. From that point on, the Allied supply position improved dramatically. The Germans quickly realized they had to recapture Antwerp.

To the south of Montgomery, Patton pushed steadily through Lorraine, south of Metz, throughout the fall. In the center of the line the advance of two U.S. armies through the difficult country east of Liége in Belgium met with extremely stubborn German resistance, particularly around Aachen and in the Hürtgen forest.

Although the Germans slowed the Allied advance in these areas, to the south of the Ardennes Allied troops made great gains. Despite bitter fighting around Metz in September, Strasbourg was taken by November 23. A German army was holding out in a pocket around Colmar, still the Allied forces on either side of the pocket had reached the west bank of the Rhine.

The Battle of the Bulge

The scene was subsequently set for the last major German offensive of the war. It became known as the Battle of the Bulge as the first German attacks created a bulge or dent in the Allied line. No one in the Allied command thought it likely that an attack through the heavily wooded Ardennes was likely in the depths of winter. That sector of the Allied line was considered "quiet" and the units there were spread thinly.

Hitler aimed to punch through this part of the line and split the British and American forces. Even at this late stage, and knowing the Allied commitment to the total defeat of Germany, he believed the British and Americans would beg for peace. However, several of Hitler's generals had serious doubts about the operation.

AFRICAN AMERICANS

African Americans played a major role in America's war effort during World War II. At home African Americans worked in factories producing the weapons and munitions that soldiers needed to fight. However, many African Americans faced work discrimination. A Philip Randolph, a labor leader, planned a protest march in Washington in July 1941 to protest against the discrimination. However, President Roosevelt introduced the first ever Fair Employment order shortly before the march was to take place, prohibiting discrimination in war-related industries.

Many African Americans, more than 500,000, played a much more direct role by fighting in the front lines. Leading personalities of the day, including heavyweight boxer Joe Louis, were recruited to encourage other African Americans to enlist. However, military units were not integrated and the officers of black units were often white. It was not until 1949 that African Americans and whites were allowed to serve together.

One of the most famous African American units was the 332nd Fighter Group, which trained at Tuskegee, Alabama, and served in southern Europe. The group's pilots shot down over 400 enemy aircraft.

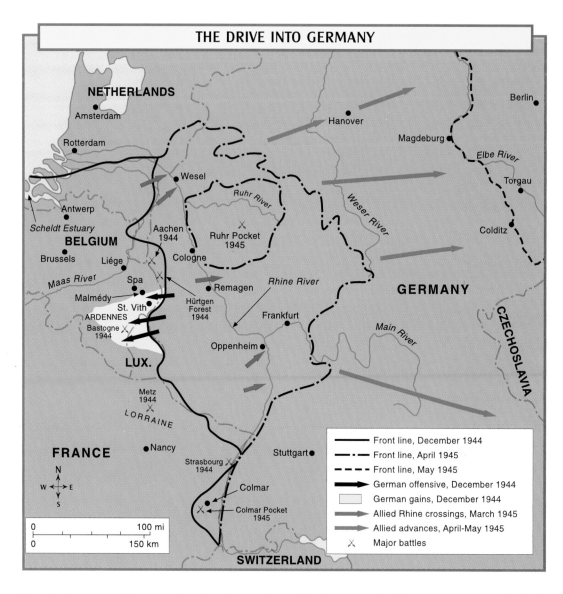

THE DRIVE INTO GERMANY

NETHERLANDS
Amsterdam
Rotterdam
Antwerp
Scheldt Estuary
BELGIUM
Brussels   Liége
Maas River   Spa
Malmédy
St. Vith
ARDENNES
Bastogne
1944
LUX.
Metz
1944
LORRAINE
FRANCE   Nancy
N
W   E
S
0   100 mi
0   150 km

Wesel
Ruhr River
Aachen
1944   Ruhr Pocket
1945
Cologne
Remagen   Rhine River
Hürtgen
Forest
1944   Frankfurt
Oppenheim
Strasbourg
1944
Colmar
Colmar Pocket
1945

Hanover
Magdeburg
Weser River
GERMANY
Main River
Stuttgart

Berlin
Elbe River
Torgau
Colditz
CZECHOSLAVIA

Front line, December 1944
Front line, April 1945
Front line, May 1945
German offensive, December 1944
German gains, December 1944
Allied Rhine crossings, March 1945
Allied advances, April-May 1945
Major battles

SWITZERLAND

The final stages of the campaign fought against Germany from late 1944 until the British and Americans met up with the Red Army along the Elbe River in May 1945.

During November 24 German divisions were assembled in secrecy. The attack came on December 16 and the Germans achieved complete surprise. They overran the U.S. divisions on a 60-mile (96-km) sector of the front. The defenders were troubled by bad weather, which grounded aircraft, but U.S. units to the north and south of the German advance held firm.

Allied reinforcements were rushed into the battle and fought with great heroism to defend the vital road junctions at St. Vith and Bastogne, slowing the German advance. As the German forces moved behind the Allied line they were plagued by the problem that had dogged their operations for months—fuel shortages. The Germans came close to capturing the massive fuel dump south of Spa, but were driven back. Their vehicles began to run out of fuel. Allied reinforcements supported by aircraft began to push back the German attackers. Bastogne was relieved on December 26. By the end of January 1945 all the early German gains had been lost. Hitler's last gamble had failed.

The final attacks

The Allies now continued their advance to the Rhine River. Hitler continued to refuse any withdrawal behind the Rhine, condemning many of his remaining troops to surrender. The Colmar Pocket was captured by February 9. On March 7, the Allies had a stroke of luck—they captured the bridge over the Rhine at Remagen intact and U.S. units were able to enter German territory. The Rhine was again breached on the 22nd when Patton's troops crossed the river at Oppenheim. Montgomery crossed the Rhine at Wesel on the 23rd.

Effective German resistance ended after the Allies crossed the Rhine. As the Allied armies drove toward Berlin, the Ruhr, the center of German industry, was captured by April 18, along with 300,000 German troops. By the beginning of May, U.S. and British forces had reached the Elbe River, where they met the Red Army. Berlin had already fallen on the 2nd. Germany formally surrendered on May 8, VE–Day (Victory in Europe Day).

British artillery pounds the German-occupied east bank of the Rhine River shortly before General Montgomery's forces crossed this last natural barrier blocking their entry into the heart of Germany, March 1945.

NAZI GERMANY DEFEATED

In January 1944, many of the German troops on the Eastern Front were enduring their fourth winter of the war, most believing that there would be no new offensive by the Red Army until the late spring. Few Germans held any hopes that the new year would bring them victory, despite what Hitler believed. Since 1941 the quality of the Soviet Union's generals had improved greatly and the Red Army, with its seemingly endless reserves of manpower and equipment, was now a formidable fighting machine.

Soviet forces launched new offensives along the whole length of the Eastern Front early in 1944. In the north an assault around Leningrad pushed the German forces away from the city. The winter offensive in the Ukraine launched the First and Second Ukrainian Fronts (large armies) on a southwestern advance, capturing Zhitomir and encircling 100,000 German troops near Korsun. The southwestern Ukrainian town formed the center of the Cherkassy Pocket. The six German divisions trapped at Cherkassy fought desperately to break out. General Erich von Manstein sacrificed an estimated 20,000 men and all his tank reserves in his failed attempt to relieve them.

With Korsun taken, the Soviets crossed the Bug and Dniester Rivers, before advancing steadily toward Romania. They entered Romanian territory, the location of Hitler's vital oil fields, on March 26. On April 8, a massive Soviet offensive was launched against the German armies trapped in the Crimea (see map on

A lone German soldier awaits the next attack by Soviet forces in the summer of 1944. He is surrounded by destroyed Russian armor, including a single T-34 (left) and a pair of British-built Valentine tanks. Both Britain and the United States supplied the Soviets with large amounts of weapons and equipment.

MORALE AND THE WILL TO WIN

Wars are won by soldiers and a soldier's will to win depends on many things, including how he or she feels–his or her morale. Morale can be affected by many influences. For example, a well-trained, well-equipped soldier with confidence in his officers is likely to triumph over a poorly-trained, badly-equipped soldier who lacks belief in his superiors.

Morale can be improved by contact with home, such as letters from loved ones, and entertainment. All of the countries involved in World War II tried to increase their soldiers' morale with various types of entertainment. Stage shows, movies, radio broadcasts, and personal visits from major stars were all used to boost morale.

Great Hollywood stars of the era, people like Marlene Dietrich and Bob Hope, often visited the front to perform for the troops. Some movie stars, such as U.S. actor Jimmy Stewart, joined the armed forces.

The American USO (United Services Organizations) troupes entertained units at the front and stars such as the Andrews Sisters gave performances. The British had ENSA (Entertainments National Service Organization), which visited units to perform shows.

page 20). Sevastopol, the Crimea's main city, was captured on May 12. These Soviet successes enraged Hitler, who lost no time in replacing several senior generals, including Manstein.

Despite now being faced with a war on two fronts following the Allied invasion of Normandy in northern France on June 6, Hitler refused to consider a strategy of withdrawing to more defendable positions on the Eastern Front. Not an inch was to be given up without a fight. He still commanded forces in the East, at least on paper, totaling some three million men, 3,000 tanks, and 3,000 aircraft. However, the Russians could field well over six million men, supported by 8,000 tanks, and 13,000 aircraft.

German forces crushed

When the Soviet command launched the summer offensive of 1944, there could be little doubt about its outcome. In the north two huge Soviet armies attacked Army Group North, forcing it back toward the Baltic states. But the major thrust of the offensive came in the center. Code-named Operation Bagration, this was designed to clear German forces from Byelorussia on the western border of the Soviet Union and place the Red Army within striking distance of Warsaw, the Polish capital. The attack

The final stages of the war on the Eastern Front, from early 1944 to May 1945, saw a series of offensives by the Red Army. Overwhelmed by sheer weight of numbers, the German armies began to collapse. The final battle of the war was for Berlin, the German capital. The city, which was virtually flattened, fell in early May.

THE FINAL BATTLES IN THE EAST

began on June 22, punching toward Minsk. The city was taken on July 3. The German forces in the sector crumpled under the hammerblows delivered by the Red Army. The Soviet advance continued toward the Polish border. Despite a temporary check to the Soviet advance east of Warsaw, Red Army units had reached the upper Vistula River by August 7.

The focus of the offensive now switched to the south. Romania was invaded on August 20 and surrendered soon after. Meanwhile, in Poland, a heroic uprising by the Polish Home Army in Warsaw, which had begun on August 1, was finally crushed by the Germans at the end of September. Soviet troops in Yugoslavia were aided by Yugoslavian guerrillas in the capture of Belgrade, the capital, on October 20. By the end of the month Soviet forces in the north had entered East Prussia and were fighting on German soil for the first time. With winter approaching, however, Soviet offensive operations were halted.

THE HOLOCAUST

As the Allies closed in on Germany during 1945, they began to uncover the true nature of Nazi Germany. Dotted across Germany and areas occupied by the Germans, the Allies uncovered death camps, where those considered to be "racially inferior" to the Germans were being systematically brutalized and murdered on a huge scale. Among those singled out for death were Jews, gypsies, and other peoples from Eastern Europe. This was the Holocaust.

The ordered program of mass extermination, known as the "Final Solution" was agreed on by senior Nazis at a meeting in a Berlin suburb in January 1942. Those present at the meeting, the Wannsee Conference, discussed "the final solution to the Jewish question." It was decided that some people, usually the very young, very old, the sick, and the mentally disturbed, would be exterminated immediately. Others, the stronger ones, would be sent to concentration camps, where they would work for Germany. Many perished through overwork, starvation, sickness, and the brutality of their guards. Many also died in pointless medical experiments

Those sent to extermination camps were shot at first, but this method of killing was considered too slow, so a new method was developed. People were herded into gas chambers, which had been disguised as showers. They were locked inside and a poisonous gas was dropped in, usually through the roof. Bodies were either buried in mass graves or burned in ovens.

The total number of victims of the Holocaust will never be known, but is probably a figure of more than six million.

The final Soviet offensive of the war in Europe was launched on January 12, 1945. Overwhelmed by the sheer weight of men and armor, the Germans fell apart. Zhukov, hero of Kursk, reached the Oder River on January 31. A last-ditch German counterattack was launched, but crushed. Crossing the Austrian frontier on March 20, Soviet forces took Vienna, the Austrian capital, on April 15. Berlin was the next objective.

The three Soviet armies that began the final attack on Berlin on April 16 were more than a match for the old men, boys, and shattered German units left to defend the capital of the Third Reich. The Red Army had encircled Berlin by April 25, the same day that U.S. forces met up with Soviet troops at Torgau on the Elbe River. The Battle of Berlin was fought from house to house. It was not until May 2 that the fighting ended. Hitler had already committed suicide in his bunker in Berlin.

THE DEFEAT
OF JAPAN

By the opening months of 1945, it was clear that American military might, backed by the country's industrial power, would defeat the Japanese. The Japanese were short of soldiers, equipment, and supplies. Japan was also suffering the impact of a massive strategic bombing campaign that was flattening most of its major cities and killing hundreds of thousands. Yet, the Japanese seemed no nearer surrendering. Soldiers were fighting on despite the odds and preferring death to captivity. U.S. generals and politicians began to wonder if an amphibious attack on Japan would lead to far too many casualties.

Despite these high-level concerns, U.S. forces continued to island-hop ever closer to Japan. With the Philippines secure, the Americans pondered which islands should be their next target. The final two major amphibious assaults of the war in the Pacific were against Iwo Jima and Okinawa, outlying Japanese islands. These attacks would mark the first time that Allied forces had fought on Japanese territory.

The battles for both Iwo Jima and Okinawa were extraordinarily bloody, the two most costly in terms of the number of soldiers killed of the whole Pacific campaign. The heavy losses on Okinawa, in particular, persuaded many in the American high command that the use of the newly developed atomic weapons was the only way to end the conflict quickly.

U.S. Marines take cover as the explosive charge they have placed against a Japanese position on Iwo Jima detonates.

Iwo Jima was the target for an amphibious assault on February 19, 1945. Delays in mounting the assault gave the defenders opportunity to construct a large number of fortifications. Tunnels, trenches, and strongpoints littered the island. The U.S. invasion fleet moved the Fifth Amphibious Corps into position on the night of February 18. The landings were preceded by a mass naval bombardment. However, the Marines were met with heavy fire as they came ashore, taking 2,420 casualties on the first day alone.

The 23,000-strong force of Japanese defenders held out until March 20. Mount Suribachi, the strongest Japanese defensive position on Iwo Jima, was finally taken on February 23—the raising of the U.S. flag on its summit remains one of the most famous images of the war.

By the end of March the airfields on the island were ready to deal with U.S. aircraft involved in the strategic bombing of Japan, but American casualties had been high. Over 6,800 Marines had been killed in the fighting and more than 18,000 had been wounded. Only 216 Japanese prisoners were taken . Admiral Nimitz's comment about his troops at Iwo Jima that "uncommon valor was a common virtue" was very true.

Closing in on Japan

Many of the men who had endured the hell of Iwo Jima were part of the force that set sail in late March to assault Okinawa, the last Japanese stronghold in the Pacific outside Japan itself. The assault was the largest and most ambitious of the entire Pacific campaign. A massive naval bombardment of Okinawa began on March 23 and was matched by a huge air campaign. The actual invasion began on April 1, 1945.

KAMIKAZE

Kamikaze is a Japanese word meaning "divine wind." It refers to a typhoon that sank an invasion fleet that was trying to invade Japan in 1281. In the latter part of the war in the Pacific, it was used to describe the Japanese pilots who willingly undertook suicide missions against U.S. vessels. Kamikaze attacks became increasingly common after the naval Battle of Leyte Gulf in October 1944, and during the course of the war dozens of U.S. ships were sunk by suicide pilots.

It was impressed upon the Japanese volunteer pilots that they were performing an honorable task worthy of the emperor. Before take-off the pilots would be ceremoniously honored at their air bases. Most of the aircraft used in the suicide attacks were standard Japanese single-seat fighters.

These were loaded with bombs and fuel to maximize the damage as they plummeted at steep angles into Allied ships, whose only defense was to send up a wall of flak into the dive-path.

Later in the war the Japanese used rocket-powered piloted missiles that were carried near to the target by larger aircraft and then flown under their own power. The Americans named the machine "Baka," meaning fool, because most were destroyed by U.S. fighter cover before reaching a target.

By early 1945 the Japanese had been forced out of many of the islands they had captured in 1941–42. U.S. troops launched two major amphibious attacks on Iwo Jima and Okinawa, both of which were successful, but casualties were heavy. Plans were laid to invade Japan itself, but these proved unnecessary. The dropping of atomic bombs on Hiroshima and Nagasaki in August led to Japan's unconditional surrender. In the final weeks of the war, the Red Army also took the opportunity to evict the Japanese from Manchuria.

THE DEFEAT OF JAPAN

Legend:
— Japanese occupied areas, August 1944
- - - Japanese occupied areas, August 1945
✕ Major battles
Atomic bomb raids, August 1945
→ Soviet offensive, August, 1945

Four U.S. divisions were landed but, unlike at Iwo Jima, they met no immediate opposition as they came ashore. Most of Okinawa's 130,000 defenders had withdrawn to strong defensive positions in the south of the island.

Japanese suicide attacks

U.S. troops reached these positions in the second half of April and were soon engaged in bitter fighting. On May 3, the Japanese launched a massive but unsuccessful counterattack on Okinawa. In the seas around Okinawa, kamikaze suicide aircraft attacks were launched against the American fleet. In all, 21 vessels were sunk and another 43 were put out of action by the Japanese aircraft that were deliberately crashed into them.

The Japanese navy was also involved in the suicide attacks. One battleship, the *Yamato*, which was the largest ever built, headed for the U.S. warships off Okinawa on a one-way journey. It never reached the U.S. fleet. It was sunk by torpedoes and bombs on April 7. Over 2,400 of the *Yamato*'s crew went down with their ship. U.S. casualties in the battle were 84 men.

On Okinawa itself U.S. ground troops launched an assault on May 11 in dreadful weather conditions. They drove the Japanese back to the hilly ground at the southern tip of the island. Reaching the hills on June 1, the Americans made a final attack that eventually overcame the enemy, who had literally fought to the last man. Even Japanese civilians preferred to commit suicide by jumping off steep cliffs to surrender, despite U.S., pledges to treat them fairly. The fighting ended on the 22nd. Okinawa had been a bloodbath. The Japanese had around 120,000 dead. U.S. casualties totaled over 12,000 killed and nearly 37,000 wounded.

The dawn of atomic war

With the capture of Okinawa, which was close to Japan, the final phase of the U.S. bombing offensive against Japan began. Throughout February and March, bombers had already been attacking Japanese industrial cities. On March 9–10 a raid on Tokyo, the capital, left much of the city in ruins.

U.S. commanders prepared for an invasion of Japan. The plan involved two separate assaults, one in November and the second in March 1946. However, events back in the United States were to make such plans unnecessary.

U.S. equipment rolls ashore on Okinawa from large amphibious assault ships. The U.S. Navy took a pounding during the invasion. More than 35 ships were sunk and over 360 suffered varying degrees of damage.

HIROSHIMA AND NAGASAKI

On August 6, 1945, the U.S. Air Force B-29 Superfortress *Enola Gay* unleashed the most powerful and destructive weapon ever seen on the Japanese city of Hiroshima, the atomic bomb. The Germans, British, and Americans had been developing atomic weapons for a number of years, but the Americans were the first to use an atomic bomb. The bomb dropped on Hiroshima was nicknamed "Fat Man." It was produced by Robert Oppenheimer and the team working on the secret Los Alamos project.

Nearly 80,000 people died as an immediate result of the explosion and 75 percent of the mainly wooden buildings in the city were destroyed by blast or fire. In subsequent weeks and months a further 70,000 succumbed to the effects of radiation sickness and burns.

Three days after the Hiroshima explosion, "Little Boy" was exploded in the sky above the Japanese industrial center of Nagasaki. Forty thousand people died and nearly half the city was destroyed. Japan offered to surrender on the following day.

The ruins of Hiroshima after the dropping of the atomic bomb.

General Douglas MacArthur signs the official Japanese surrender document on the U.S.S. Missouri *in Tokyo Bay, September 2, 1945. Standing behind MacArthur are U.S. General Jonathan Wainwright, (left) who was captured in the Philippines in 1942, and General A.E. Percival, who surrendered the British forces defending Singapore to the Japanese also in 1942. Both men still show the effects of several years of poor treatment in Japanese prison camps.*

On July 16, 1945, the world's first atomic bomb was exploded at Alamogordo, New Mexico. After the explosion of this atomic bomb, a debate raged through the U.S. government about using such weapons. Harry S Truman, who had become president after the sudden death of Roosevelt in April, made the decision to use the weapon. He, backed by the other Allies, demanded an immediate Japanese surrender at the end of July. That demand was ignored. On August 6, an atomic bomb was exploded over Hiroshima. The devastation that it wrought, and an atomic bomb attack on Nagasaki on August 9, forced the Japanese to offer surrender on August 10. However, there are people who still believe Truman's decision was morally wrong.

The final cost

The official surrender of Japan on September 2 ended World War II. The Allied victory had been bought at a very high cost. The war's military casualties totaled 15 million dead and many more wounded. Civilian deaths, including the six million European Jews murdered in Hitler's death camps, are estimated at between 26 and 34 million. Both Germany's and Japan's leaders were tried and many convicted of war crimes. However, the horrors of World War II were not enough to stop future conflicts.

GLOSSARY

antitank gun A type of artillery designed specifically to destroy armored vehicles, such as tanks. Such guns fired shells designed to pierce armor plate. They were either towed or fitted to the modified chassis of a tank.

armored division The most powerful fighting formation of World War II. A typical armored division contained around 15,000 personnel. At its heart were several tank units. However, a division also contained infantry units, artillery batteries, antitank gunners and reconnaissance units.

ground-attack aircraft A specialized type of aircraft. Equipped with bombs, rockets, and machine guns, these one- or two-engined aircraft acted closely with ground units. Their role, as a type of "flying artillery," was to hit enemy targets threatening to stop an advance by friendly forces. They also ranged beyond the immediate battlefield seeking out "targets of opportunity," such as enemy bases or troop-carrying trains.

landing craft Used chiefly during attacks on enemy-occupied coasts, these vessels came in a variety of sizes and shapes. Some were built to carry infantrymen, while others transported heavier equipment, such as tanks, to the invasion beach. Most had doors in their bows that either swung open or simply dropped down.

mortar A type of light, short-range cannon consisting of a circular metal tube and a two-legged support. Shells are dropped into the tube and flung out in a plunging arc. Several shells a minute can be fired, and mortars are particularly useful for firing over obstacles, such as a hill.

paratrooper A highly trained soldier who is dropped into a war area by parachute or landed in a glider. Paratroopers are used to seize vital targets by surprise in advance of the main army. They are usually lightly equipped. All U.S. paratroopers volunteer to be members of such units.

self-propelled gun A type of mobile artillery that can be moved under its own power rather than being pulled by another vehicle. In World War II self-propelled guns consisted of a modified tank chassis onto which the gun itself had been placed in a high-sided but open-topped turret.

strategic bombing A term denoting the use of long-range bombers to smash an enemy's ability to wage war by destroying his industries and transportation systems. In World War II, the Allies carried out such a policy of round-the-clock bombing against Germany from 1943, although some historians doubt whether the attacks had any major impact on Germany's war-fighting capacity.

BIBLIOGRAPHY

Note: *An asterisk (*) denotes a Young Adult title.*

*Altman, Linda J. *Genocide: The Systematic Killing of a People.* Enslow, 1995

Breuer, William B. *Unexplained Mysteries of World War II.* John Wiley and Sons Inc., 1997

*Carlson, Lewis H. *We Were Each Other's Prisoners—An Oral History of World War II American and German Prisoners.* Basic Books, 1997

Commager, Henry Steele. *The Story of the Second World War.* Brassey's, 1998

*Drez, Ronald J. *Voices of D-Day—The Story of the Allied Invasion Told by Those Who Were There.* Louisiana State University Press, 1994

*Jones, Catherine. *Navajo Code Talkers: Native American Heroes.* Tudor, 1998

Lucas, James. *War on the Eastern Front—The German Soldier in Russia, 1941–1945.* Stackpole Books, 1998

*McKissack, Patricia and McKissack, Fredrick. *Red-Tail Angels: The Story of the Tuskegee Airmen of World War II.* Walker, 1995

*Ross, Stewart. *World War II.* Steck-Vaughn Company, 1996

INDEX

ACKNOWLEDGMENTS

Cover (main picture) Robert Hunt Library, (inset) Robert Hunt Library; page 1 Robert Hunt Library/Imperial War Museum; page 5 Robert Hunt Library; page 7 Robert Hunt Library; page 8 Robert Hunt Library; page 9 Robert Hunt Library; page 10 Robert Hunt Library; page 13 TRH Pictures; page 15 Robert Hunt Library/Imperial War Museum; page 16 Robert Hunt Library; page 18 Robert Hunt Library; page 19 Robert Hunt Library; page 21 AKG Photo, London; page 22 Robert Hunt Library; page 24 Robert Hunt Library; page 25 Robert Hunt Library; page 26 Robert Hunt Library/Imperial War Museum; page 29 Robert Hunt Library; page 30 Robert Hunt Library/ U.S. National Archives; page 32 Robert Hunt Library; page 33 Robert Hunt Library; page 35Robert Hunt Library; page 36 Robert Hunt Library; page 38 Robert Hunt Library/Imperial War Museum; page 40 Robert Hunt Library; page 41 Robert Hunt Library; page 43 Robert Hunt Library; page 45 Robert Hunt Library; page 46 Robert Hunt Library/U.S. Air Force; page 48 Robert Hunt Library/Imperial War Museum; page 49 Robert Hunt Library; page 50 Robert Hunt Library; page 53 Robert Hunt Library; page 54 Robert Hunt Library; page 55 Robert Hunt Library; page 56 Robert Hunt Library/Imperial War Museum; page 58 Robert Hunt Library, U.S. National Archives; page 60 Robert Hunt Library/U.S.A.. National Archives; page 62 Robert Hunt Library/U.S. National Archives; page 63 Robert Hunt Library/ Imperial War Museum; page 64 Robert Hunt Library/U.S. National Archives; page 67 Robert Hunt Library/Imperial War Museum; page 68 Robert Hunt Library; page 72 Robert Hunt Library/U.S. Marine Corps; page 75 Robert Hunt Library/ U.S. Navy; page 76 Robert Hunt Library/U.S. Army; page 77 Robert Hunt Library/ U.S. Navy.